IF I DIDN'T

START WRITING

I WOULD NEVER

FINISH

...

WORK

PLAY

PASSION

. . .

JIM CLARK WRITES HIS MEMOIRS OF

MAKING FRIENDS *with* CANDY

and her journal of life and love

JIM CLARK

. . .

This is a work of non-fiction. Some names and other details, however have been changed.

Published by Clark & Company
Layout / Design by www.juststay.com
Cover Photography by Jim Clark

www.MakingFriendsWithCandy.com

ISBN 978-0-615-43775-0

CELEBRATE

EVERY DAY

AS IF IT WAS

YOUR LAST

X O

INTRODUCTION

If you only read this introduction I want you to know that things do happen for a reason, even if we do not know why. I believe people are put into our lives and it's up to us to make the most of those encounters. And, that you can find love within the most troubling times or darkest moments in your life, as well as in the lives of others. This is the story of a chance meeting and my commitment to do what that voice in my head, as well as my heart, said was the right thing to do.

I would not wish the last year of Candy's life on anyone. She lived through "hell on earth", the death of her unborn child, being diagnosed with cancer, then discovering more about herself, her "real" friends, and the family she never knew she had.

I was blessed to come into Candy's life and I wouldn't trade it for anything in the world. I hope you enjoy reading my story about making friends with Candy, a view from down the street online. And, if you are as lucky as I was, you will learn something new about yourself or enjoy a good read as an observer looking in.

DEDICATION

I want to dedicate this book to "friends". Your friends and mine, the people who are there for you when you need them and there without even having to ask.

To my family, of course, because without them I would not have become the person I am today. They taught me to be kind to people no matter what. Even if others had different views, different beliefs, or even looked different than you, we are all human and should treat each other with respect and kindness.

To my AD3 family, because having fun is a big part of living. Work. Play. Passion. Love you guys! ...

And to Candy, for letting me into her life and sharing her precious time with me, making me smile, loving me, and teaching me more about myself. Sending much love to you up there in heaven looking down on all of us.

TABLE OF CONTENTS

THOUGHTS 13

CHAPTER 1 .... **ADD ME?** 15

CHAPTER 2 ....**GETTING TO KNOW CANDY** 19

CHAPTER 3 ....**ON LINE WORLD** 23

CHAPTER 4 ....**PEOPLE AROUND CANDY** 29

CHAPTER 5 ....**THE WORLD OF CANCER** 45

CHAPTER 6 ....**MOTHER'S DAY** 57

CHAPTER 7 ....**ESCAPE FROM REALITY** 61

CHAPTER 8 .... **VIDEO BROADCASTS** 75

CHAPTER 9 ....**PHONE CALLS & VOICE MAIL** 81

CHAPTER 10 .... **THE MUSIC & VIDEOS** 87

CHAPTER 11 .... **AD 3 - TATTOOS** 95

CHAPTER 12 ....**FAMILY** 99

CHAPTER 13 .... **FINAL DAYS** 107

CHAPTER 14 .... **MESSAGES, E-MAILS, & PHOTOS** 115

CHAPTER 15 ....**ANOTHER DAY IN "CANDYLAND"** 155

CHAPTER 16 ....**SHARING CANDY WITH STRANGERS** 173

CHAPTER 17 .... **AFTER THOUGHTS** 177

CONCLUSION 189

AUTHOR'S NOTE 191

THE JOURNAL ....**CANDY'S GIFT TO ME** 193

THOUGHTS

When I decided to share Candy's story as a book I had no idea where to begin. But I knew if I didn't start writing I would never finish. The hardest thing for me to do is to type or write with tears in my eyes, tears of sadness and happiness. They make it hard to focus on the commitment I made to share this story with others, but I will make it happen.

The next thing I had to figure out was the best way to present this story. I want you to get as much out of it as I did, and I want you to be able to read Candy's journal just as I read it the first time. The journal is typed at the end of the book. Some names are not included.

As I'm writing, I am going to insert photos, e-mails, messages, and whatever comes to mind to show you more of my unforgettable three and a half month experience with Candy. Some of the e-mails, comments, and messages have not been edited as I would like to preserve their essence.

I hope reading this book doesn't make you sad, but instead, helps you appreciate what we are each blessed with while on this earth. Also, that we should cherish the precious time we have by spending it with the people close to us and not take it for granted.

CHAPTER 1

ADD ME?

It was around the middle of April when I was checking messages on the social media web site, Facebook. I read a friend's comment and noticed a photo of a blonde girl with a nice smile and a cute hat. So, being the curious person I am, I clicked on her photo to see her profile. Her name was Candy Angel Christmas. The first thing I thought was "yeah right, that's her real name." Then, still being curious to know more about her, I clicked the "add friend" button.

A couple of weeks passed by and I had forgotten about the friend request. Then, on May 4th I saw a status posted by my new friend Candy, who added me on April 29th. The status stated: *"To my sweet little friend who sent me the messages today. I love you. I really do but please let me clarify this for you I HAVE CANCER! CANCER DOES NOT HAVE ME! Don't count me out just yet. I've got my gloves on and I'm fighting. Another round of chemo tomorrow is just another step to my recovery."*

When I saw this I thought to myself: "if I see her in the chat section online I will ask her how she was doing". It didn't take long because almost as soon as I finish my thought she was online. I clicked on her name to pop up the chat window. What do I say? She doesn't know me from anyone. Oh well, what do I have to lose? I say / text: "hi, how was your day?" and waited for a reply. She said: *"hi"* followed by *"it was ok, as good as it could be"* and we talked more about the cancer treatment and the people at the doctor's office. Then we talked about the music being played there, she called it *"funeral home"* music. I suggested that she should bring in her own music next time. She said that wouldn't be a bad idea.

The following days I would check to see if Candy was online so I could say hi. I didn't catch her for a couple of days and was too shy to make a comment on her page. I decided to send her a message and let her know that I hoped the treatments were going as well as could be. She sent a message back and said she was *"ok"*. I checked in from time to time to see if I could help her with anything.

CHAPTER 2

GETTING TO KNOW CANDY

After talking through the chat area with Candy a few times I really started to like her spunky personality. She is a little bit of a smart ass like me, but with a bit of "southern girl" thrown in on top. She didn't mind voicing her opinion on how she felt about something or someone. She would tell someone if they were being an ass or just plain mean to people. She said this about herself: *"I am just me. A far cry from amazing. I'm a little complex and confusing at times, but that's just who I am... if you want to know the real me... hang on, fasten your seatbelts...it's gonna be a bumpy ride!"* I didn't know the journey I was about to begin by just meeting her.

One evening we were talking online about our families. I mentioned how my sister had been in an abusive relationship, and I wished she had never gotten into it. Candy asked me if I wanted to see a picture. I told her that I saw her profile pictures and others she had in albums online. Then she said: *"no, my police photo"*. I remember thinking "what has this girl done?" and "who am I talking to?" Curious me types back: "sure send it to me." I was talking to a few people online that evening at the same time as I normally do, but when I get Candy's photo I became speechless. I told the other people I was talking with that I have to go, and I would talk to them later. I went back to my message which included Candy's photo. The text underneath said: *"show her this... I was five minutes from dying when I got to the hospital"*. She said the picture was taken after she had been brutality beaten by the man she had been in a relationship with for two years.

Shortly after I text her "omg". She said she shouldn't have sent it to me. I told her it was ok and that I was really glad she lived through it. She said: *"thanks, but my unborn daughter was not so lucky."* I didn't know what to say. She went on to tell me that her friend Jazmyn luckily came by the house before she had died, and took her to the hospital. I told her that karma would get the people who did this to her, she told me that it had already happened. I said: "really, wow". She told me that her boyfriend had gone to prison and his cell mate killed him there.

I questioned myself: "what have I gotten myself into?" and at the same time: "what should I say next, should I keep talking to this girl? is she real or not?" But that voice inside my head said not to worry because I could quit anytime I wanted to. We talked a little bit longer about random stuff and then said we would talk again soon. I told her that I would be online tomorrow and signed off.

"Dimples, silly hat and all... I'm here... if you don't *like the fact that I am, move on... it's called delete. Use it. I still have those who love me even though some of you have tried to make me leave.* Not going anywhere... just yet."

This was Candy's profile picture the first time I talked to her online.

CHAPTER 3

ONLINE WORLD

What's it all about? Facebook, MySpace, Skype, IChat, Yahoo! Messenger, chat rooms, virtual worlds like Second Life, Vside, and many others are all available for people to communicate and have fun. They can be good or bad experiences depending on the people who are there. I have been dancing with friends online, introduced to their friends, and meet some of them in person later. I continue to meet people online, create new friendships, and enjoy seeing them grow. I have also been insulted and treated like I wouldn't have treated anyone in real life. I guess it's ok in their minds to treat others bad online 'cause they don't consider it real. I don't know. Even though I didn't really know Candy, up to this point I have had a positive experience with her. However, I still had friends who checked in with me to make sure I was not falling for a fake person. They didn't want me to be taken advantage of. I appreciate my friends for looking out for me and I hope they continue to do so.

Candy had people tell her that she was not a real person because of her profile photos. Her photographs prior to her cancer were burned in the fireplace by her boyfriend. The night of "hell on earth", as she used to refer to the night he almost beat her to death. She used modeling photos from a online clothing catalog she had worked for. Here are some of the comments when questioned if she was real and a few of the photos she had been using:

Candy ~ *"If you have a question about whether I am real just ask my real friends who know. Ric he's real, Rachel she's real, Jim he's real. If there are any doubts just do us both a favor and delete me and block me please. I'm too tired for your questions and your games. Don't worry about Karma and I."*

Candy ~ *"You see, God trumps karma on any given day. And He alone is my judge. Have a blessed life. God knows I'm real ask Him! or are you not on speaking terms??? And leave my friend Rachel alone!"*

Rae ~ "Candy ignorance lies in the face of those who have trouble with their own lives. When you are unhappy with your own life it's easier to attack others who have one. You are surrounded by people who love you. Don't worry about me honey. I have learned to ignore the ignorant. I love you."

Jim ~ "oh oh ask me, pick me, pick me and I will give you a piece of my mind about Candy, it may be a little bit to real for you but I'll let you have it anyway... just saying :)"

Ernest ~ "i know you're real. heck, i'm looking right at you!!"

But it even got worse than that. When Candy was suffering from the side effects of cancer treatments and in extreme pain, she had people tell her to "go ahead and die already". What kind of human beings are these? Who would say something like that? I hope they did take time to reflect on what they had said. People should think about what they are saying at least twice before they press the "send" button.

After starting her chemo treatments Candy knew her hair was going to fall out. It had started to come out in her brush and instead of being reminded about it every time she saw her reflection, Candy and Rae decided to cut it all off. They scheduled a day, got the scissors and clippers together and some hats to wear after.

Candy changes her status to reflect what's going on in her life. May 8th her status reads: *"Well enjoy the photos because Goldilock's hair will be saying goodbye within the hour. If its just gotta go ...it's going my way... it's not gonna be a pretty sight but wth.. I have pictures! lol ... Pass along the hats please this girl's gonna need 'em. I know bald is beautiful on you men ... but this is gonna take some getting used to. xo ;)"*

Candy ~ *Pacing the floor, jumping up and down, Waiting for Rae , listening for the sound of the clippers and the snap of the scissors, and the gentle fall of these lovely locks hitting the floor.. Let's get it done. Let's complete this page in my book today. Hats layed out to choose from which will it be? I'm just thankful this is one part of this journey where I am in control. ;)*

Larry ~ It's just for a while ,,,, :)

Candy ~ *I've made peace with it Larry. I'm ok.. hopefully my head wont look like a road map lol or a bowling ball lol*

Raquel ~ >hugs< Ms. ... ... Meow LPK

Rae ~ You controlled it we took our time and the end result is simply mahvelous!

The Facebook family tends to comment when it concerns their friends and especially when someone is negative or not playing nice. Most of your friends can tell by your tone if you are having a good day or not, and will comment to try to make your day better.

The bio Candy posted on Facebook said this: *"I'm just going to be me and breathe while I'm here. No need to pretend. I'll just be who I am. I'm only here for a little while, so who needs more drama? I'm nothing special. I don't expect special treatment. I don't need your pity nor do I seek it. I'm just a girl fighting cancer and who's time is running out. So there it is. The truth. Some days I'm laughing my butt off. Other days I'm crying my eyes out. It's just how my life is...it's just my truth. I have a few incredible friends who make me smile while I'm here and that's enough for me. So, today I will just breathe and take the day as it comes.... no need for questions. And no I won't meet you. I'm not looking into the eyes of anyone else I'll have to say goodbye to. I'm sorry, I'm dealing with this the best way I can. Just breathe... it will be ok. xo"*

CHAPTER 4

PEOPLE AROUND CANDY

JAZMYN

Jazmyn was one of Candy's model friends who had convinced Candy to do some modeling herself. I believe they worked and lived together somewhere in Georgia, and that Jazmyn's family treated her as if she was one of their girls. Candy sent me a modeling picture of Jazmyn and her from a catalog that they were in to promote and sell swimwear.

Candy told me that Jazmyn could talk her into doing almost anything, including the time they got tattoos after drinking a little too much tequila. They both got butterflies tattooed on their *"tits"*, as Candy said, so they couldn't be seen when working as models.

Candy told me about the two of them going down to south Florida for an audition as QVC models. They were auditioning to promote the selling of snow blowers. When on the set, Candy told me she couldn't stop laughing thinking people in Florida *"were never going to buy snow blowers"*. She said it was a "blonde moment" and no, they didn't get the job, but had a fun time.

Jazmyn's parents were successful people and had set up savings accounts for the girls. Candy was able to fight her battle against cancer without worrying about where the money for medical bills would come from. I hope they realize they did a wonderful and thoughtful thing for her.

Sadly, Jazmyn was killed by a drunk driver in November prior to Candy's fight with cancer. Candy talked about her everyday and I know she was missed. She told me that she thought Jazmyn's soul had went into the cat at the lake house. She could feel her spirit talking to her when things were not going her way. And when Candy moved back to the beach, she thought Jazymn's spirit was in a little black bird. Candy would enjoy the visits of the bird while having breakfast on the balcony. I don't know if it was the medicines Candy was taking, or her way of coping with the stress of the situation. I can imagine a little of both.

Candy changed her status on May 23rd to say: *"I wish I could put a ladder up to heaven and bring you back for just one day, so I could know you are OK where you are now ...I miss you Jazmyn ...see you soon."*

JIMMY

I don't know Jimmy and Candy didn't talk about him to me. I feel they were very close at one time but I don't know the story behind the two of them. I did think it was ironic that he was named Jimmy and I am Jim.

RAE

Rae... wow! what to say about this lady? Where do I start? Rae did so many things for Candy. I know she misses her more than anyone on this whole earth.

I met Rae indirectly online through conversations and comments on Facebook. If I made a comment on Candy's Facebook wall, Rae would reply something through a post as well. After reading more posts from Rae to Candy I understood that she was a true caring friend. Rae had no hidden agenda and was not just typing stuff to be heard. She was there for Candy online and in the real world. She was a shoulder to lean on, cry on, and even throw up on. This was Rae's comment to Candy on April 29th - "Candy I'm a phone call away honey. You know that . I'll come running any time day or night. love you Ill check on ya ok xo".

Rae and Candy's friendship was very meaningful to each other. As friends do, they would share each others problems, try to find solutions, or at least comfort each other in the best way that they could. And it didn't stop there, Rae is still my friend and will always be one.

Candy posted a few photos and comments about some people in her life closer to the end, this is what she said about Rae: *"I couldn't have pulled through all of this without you. All the times you have run to me at a moments notice and the untold things you have done. No one could have a better friend than you. You know you are my hero! Forever and always!"*

I asked Rae a few questions about Candy, here are her responses:

When did you first meet Candy?

I don't remember exactly when it exactly was. I know it was right after she signed up for fbook. Feb.? March? My memory is bad I'm sorry.

What types of things did you guys do for fun together?

Sitting listening to her music, cooking, eating (cheesecake you know her), sometimes we would just hang out on the dock and talk when she was up to it. The majority of the time I saw her, she had just returned home from a treatment and was pretty weak. Sometimes we would drive down to the dam. She liked to listen to the rush of the water and watch it stream down or drive on the other side to the park where her favorite tree is. (I may have a photo saved of that?) Occasionally, but not very often we would take a short walk through the woods by the lake, most of the time she was just too weak for that but we did manage a few times. An occasional trip to the drive through at Mc Donald's for her famous Mocha Frappe', and sit at the Panama City Marina watching the sunset and the fishermen. Just talking. Lots of talking. Not enough talking : (.

Did you two talk on the phone late in the night when some of us were sleeping?

It was not unusual for us to be on the phone all night long after everyone was asleep. She was afraid to try to sleep or just couldn't sleep. We would talk until around 5 a.m. when it was time to get my hubby and daughter up for work and school. My phone was always on by my bed in case she just needed to talk. Sometimes it was just to listen to music together. She just needed to know someone was there. Lots of times after you went to bed she would call me. Sure do miss those times.

Doctor visits - did you go with her to them? I think you had drove her to and from some... not sure.

She always had an excuse for me not to take her to the doctor. I took her to the pharmacy but never the doctor. She kept that private. Except for the "lake people" as she called them to help her out. I never did know Pop's real name. They always took her and picked her up. I went up after she was home to check on her and help her out. Taking care of her laundry, etc. and making sure she had something to eat or drink.

What things would you like people to remember Candy most for?

Candy had the biggest heart of anyone I have ever known. She was more concerned about you and I than she was herself even when she was the sickest I'd ever seen anyone. She worried about what this was doing to everyone around her. She worried about her siblings and didn't dare let them close enough to share in her misery as she called it because she couldn't give her best to them. And that's the way she felt about you Jim. She so very much wanted to see you face to face. She cried and cried but wouldn't dare let you see her as she was because she didn't give you the best of herself as she put it. She worried about us. About hurting us. Even when she was so sick in Georgia she was giving to the children. She loved her mom. She missed Jazmyn. Although she had money she didn't see the need in material things because she had done without them for so long growing up. She never got how very beautiful she was. No matter what had been done to her, in the end she forgave them all. Every single one. I don't know that I could have done that. She didn't let anyone stand in between her and her God.

I want people to know her heart, but its impossible to describe. She loved with everything in her, the few of us who were fortunate enough to get close to her. She lived through the music. Fought through the pain. Didn't complain. Faced her battles with dignity, the one thing she said she wouldn't let them take from her. She cried more tears than one person should ever have to cry and suffered more than anyone should have to in a lifetime, but did so with grace. Every day after she lost her hair, she put on her hat or scarf like it was a crown for a princess, put a smile on her face and hid the battle raging within her from the rest of the world.

She was the most elegant, down to earth, loving, funny, brave and loveable person I have ever met. If anyone ever deserved the best life had to give it was her. And yet she said to me when I made that statement to her, she said she had the best. "I have Jim and you." she said, "And that is the very best!" In our last conversation the day she passed, her concern was for us. "You have to be ok. I have to know that you and Jim will be alright. I won't go until I know for sure. I'll keep fighting. I love you both and you just have to be ok." Even while she was so weak, she waited for me to tell her it was ok to go and wanted me to sing to her.

Candy will always be the most amazing woman I have ever known. Her many mysteries, the things she kept private, the things she couldn't remember, it was all a part of who she was. I will never forget her, the way she loved us, that incredible laugh, the way she loved music (the soundtrack to her life she said), her smile, but most of all her beautiful heart. No one or nothing can take that away from me.

BEX

Bex is a friend of Candy's who came to her aid when she needed a change. A change of scenery and surroundings is a good thing when you find out the cancer treatments are not working. And on top of that, knowing that you may only have a few months to live, what goes on in your mind can make you crazy.

I never really got to know Bex. But I knew when she flew down from Georgia to get Candy that she was a good person. When I would talk to Candy through Facebook chat, if she got up from her computer to go to the bathroom, Bex would chime in. She would type in all caps so I would know it was her instead of Candy. She would tell me to keep doing whatever I was doing because Candy was smiling and laughing out loud at times. Candy would tell me that Bex would come up to her and lick her face just for fun. Here is one of the texts from Bex:

June 8, 2010 at 12:43 pm

Re: xo HEY JIM! WANNA TRADE LICKS???...

TAGGED CANDY, YOU'RE NEXT, HAVE A GOOD TRIP ... KICK HER ASS FOR NOT EATING AGAIN TODAY! GRRR... YEP SNEAKED IN WHEN SHE WASN'T LOOKIN' SEE YA. XXXX~~~ LICK YA LATER!... ORLANDO CAN BE ORGASMIC! HAVE FUN! SHES GONNA KICK MY ASS FOR THIS LMAO ~~~

Bex, wherever you are in Georgia, I want to thank you for being there for Candy. I know it must have been very hard to do all you did for her and still go to work in the morning.

POPS

Pops was, in my mind, like Candy's grandfather. She would say that he didn't want anyone to mess with "his Candy". He must have had a big heart to take her in when she had no where to go, all at a phone calls notice. He would check on Candy during the day while running the condos at the beach. While talking to Candy online he asked if she was "talking to that guy in the computer" referring to me. She told him that I was at the sports bar *"Quig's"* in Destin, and was going to play cards. After that, he told her he knew where that place was and that he should take her there to play poker too. She laughed and told me: *"wouldn't that be a sight"*. I told her she would fit right in with the rest of us strange poker players.

On June 21st Pops delivered shrimp and oysters to Candy, who loved shrimp, and this is what she writes: *"They look good, smell great ... what to do? what to do? ... just drank that big gollywhopper of a shake... no room in the inn ..lol"* I tell her not to let them go to waste, just let me know where I needed to go and I would be right there to eat them. She told me: *"nice try, you don't give up easily".* I responded: "that's right". I am as stubborn as she is.

THE LAKE FOLKS

These people had the opportunity to enjoy Candy's good home style cooking, an honor I never had. Just as well, as I could always afford to lose a few pounds. The dishes she would make them for breakfast alone were worth the extra weight.

I remember one of the photos Candy sent me of her holding up a bass she caught while at the lake. She had cropped it to where all I could see was her from the neck down to her knees. Candy felt self conscious because of the scaring she had on her face due to the chemo treatments. It was a

good sized bass too. I found the picture, and it's right here.

RIC

I did not know Ric, but Candy thought very highly of him. She made this comment on his photo in her album of remaining friends: *"My favorite patriot. Getting me through tough times always ready to listen and kick butt when necessary. Forever encouraging me to fight another day. It goes without saying you're my hero."*

JIM - (me)

Okay, this is going to be a hard one to write. Hard because I am not used to writing or even talking about personal things. Sure, I write my observations in my blog from time to time but this is different. This is me, "Jim". A guy that got lucky by having the opportunity to be placed in a total stranger's life. I was thrown into someone's life where a good friend or many friends were needed.

Sure, I could have decided to leave the relationship at any time but the voice in my head kept saying: "this is not about you Jim, it's for you to help her anyway that you can". People would ask me: "what's in it for you?" And to that I answered: "nothing right now, but maybe helping her today may prepare me for things I might have to face in the future".

I didn't know what to expect, but I knew the "right thing to do" was to help however I could. And, with the economy where it was right now, I was not busy working on work. It was more like I was busy looking for work. With the phone calls and e-mails not getting returned, I knew work was going to be slow for a while. And on top of all that, the oil spill was not helping.

Jim meets this new girl online and gets to know her. He likes to meet new people even though he is a shy person. Well, until he gets to know you, then you can't shut him up. So I have been told. Being able to talk to a beautiful person online can't be all bad. lol... Jim talks a little bit at first then after a while can't get enough of Candy's personality and sense of humor. She is a "country girl" with enough of the city to be totally classy. She enjoys a gentlemen but is capable of opening a door for herself if needed. Candy is not afraid to give you her two cents worth on a subject. Sometimes without even asking, she will share a piece of her mind.

Enough about her, back to me - I mean "Jim". Here is some of his background. Jim was born in Greenville, South Carolina and left there when he was around 5 years old. His dad was in the Air Force and his mother worked on base from time to time.

His parents adopted two sisters when he was six years old; Kathy who was four, and Tina who was two. From there, they moved where ever the Air Force needed Jim's dad. Family was and is a good part of who we are. Being raised by both mom and dad does make a difference. Jim's brother, Michael, is born when Jim is in his late teens. With all of the moving, it was hard for Jim to get close to friends or even keep them. After retiring from the air force as an aircraft mechanic, Jim's parents decided to move to Florida. They had been stationed at Eglin Air Force Base before and enjoyed living here. They pack up the kids and Fluffy (our pet poodle) then leave Vandenburg Air Force Base in California and drive cross country. Jim's dad finds a "civilian" job and we live in Fort Walton Beach.

Jim attends school at Meigs Jr. High, Choctawhatchee High School, Okaloosa/Walton Jr. College, and then moves to Pensacola. He attends the University of West Florida, studies studio art and art education. Jim meets his future wife, Daryl Ann, in college. They get married and have two kids, Taylor and Lindsey, and life goes on.

Many years later, Jim's wife gets diagnosed with breast cancer. This is where Jim gets familiar with the deadly cancer and it's treatment. The treatment for Daryl Ann is a success, she goes for regular check ups and takes an oral medication. But as life goes on, their relationship grows apart. Jim asks for a divorce, they separate and then the marriage is over. They sell their home in Niceville and

Jim moves to a townhouse in Santa Rosa Beach with their daughter Lindsey. Taylor moves in with his girl friend and continues his pursuit of making and writing music.

I had noticed that about the same time I started AD3 and was giving people hugs instead of handshakes, it was the beginning of the end of my marriage. Sorry, it's hard to talk about yourself from the outside... I'm still working on it. But it doesn't matter, because Candy thought I was an "ok guy", and I am good with that.

Candy ~ *"No matter how bad the day is going you always make it better. All the days you take me to the beach, the place I would love to be the most. You always find a way to make me smile, and all the unspoken things.. I am honored to call you my friend and forever my hero! xo..."*

In this photo (from Candy's Facebook album): Jim Clark
Rae ~ "Certainly mine today as well."
Candy ~ "every day ;)"

CHAPTER 5

THE WORLD OF CANCER

While looking back, I came across this post from May 17th and thought I was lucky she decided to continue talking online with me and her other friends:

Candy ~ *"I have about 10 minutes left of computer time and i have to go. ia thank you for your prayers and concern. i thank rae for trying to keep everyone posted and for everything you have done for me. I thank Jimmy for loving me through this hell I've been going through. I have been told that the chemo will not work and when i leave here i will go home with hospice care."*

Candy ~ *"please don't worry just know your friendships have meant more to me than words can say. im not up to typing much but i will read your words posted for me here while I can just know that no matter what you've heaard about me. I'm real . and your friendships are treasures I will take with me when I leave."*

Candy ~ *"thank you for standing by me through all of this. i pray one day some way some how we will meet face to face and there will be no more sickness for any of us. I love you my friends. forever. if i have one wish it's that you will*

MAKING FRIENDS WITH CANDY

remember me and smile. xo"

Jasmine ~ "Be blessed".

Larry ~ "iam so sad, nothing can be said,,,,,,,,,,,,"

Rae ~ "Candy you will always be in my heart .. i'm so sorry honey. know i love you forever."

When my ex-wife was going through chemo and not happy about having to go for another treatment, I would refer to the medicine in the IV as "hummingbird food". We both enjoyed watching the hummingbirds that would visit our feeders in the backyard. I believe it made her feel a little bit better during this rough time. I told Candy this and she included it in her post on June 29th:

Candy ~ *"I made it through another day. Tomorrow, another round of the lovely hummingbird food. We don't always get what we want in life, but I'm learning to deal with what I have. Doesn't mean I have to like it, but hopefully I won't make it harder on those around me. When it's my time to go, I'll go. Until then I'll keep holding on, keep breathing, and will always NEED my true friends. Good night for now, I love you. xo"*

During Candy's chemo treatments the drug would

make her not have an appetite, or where she didn't want to eat because it would make her sick. But with that said, I felt I needed to help out any way I could. This is the day I met Rae online. Rae sent me a message and told me to keep doing whatever I was doing because Candy was happier than she had seen her in a while. I told her we were just talking and joking around like kids. Then she said: "get her to eat something". After that, I started thinking of ways to make it happen. The first thing that came to my mind was to ask Candy what she had to eat today. Her response was: *"so Rae has gotten to you?"* and I said: "Rae who?" because I hadn't met Rae until earlier that same day. I quickly changed the subject and we carried on our conversation.

Candy mentioned having to drink these multi-vitamin shakes and that she didn't like the taste of them. I told her she needed to pretend she was on the beach with a frozen cocktail with a little umbrella in it to see if that helped. It did. Candy even found some of them and put them in one of her shakes while at Bex's house.

this should be enough for a while...

I decided to make a beach photo for her with a supply of the little colorful umbrellas and post online to get (hopefully) a smile. I told her: "you have the drink... so these will make it more fun... stick it!".

MEDS

From time to time you could definitely tell when the medications were "kicking in" as we say. Candy called it *"truth serum"*. I did try to call her one time to talk when she had taken them but she e-mailed me saying: *"nope, not tonight"*. She thought it would get too crazy for me. I just laughed knowing she was feeling no pain and was having a little fun. Candy told me she didn't like to take the pain medications because they made her *"loopy"*. She didn't like the feeling of not being in control. Here is a sample of one of those days, enjoy:

Candy ~ *"is going straight to hell this morning ... but look at the company that's going with me. Gawd it feels good to not be in pain ..... !!!!!!!!!!!!!!!!!!"*

Candy ~ *"Feels more lost than a nun at an orgy!"*

Lisa ~ "I'm sure you got plenty of "Helpers" if needed..lol

Candy ~ *"lmao... omg wish i could hook you up w/this... i gotta try to behave holy crap"*

Lisa ~ "Wish i could be sittin next to ya in those chairs and whatever they're pumping u with..lol"

Candy ~ *"they showed up at 6am hooking me up at home....."*

Lisa ~ "Well, I guess it's good, You won't have to wait 5 hours.. Sorry :("

Candy ~ *"hope they come back tomorrow lol"*

Lisa ~ "Make them...:)"

Candy ~ *"I gotta get off of here for a while this stuff is like truth serum ... Bex is laughin her ass off.."*

Candy ~ *"all we need is Jim here and it would be an official party... I'd better not get any phone calls for a while either they may find out more than they want to know lol"*

Lisa ~ "I bet,,,, ur too funny today..lol"

William ~ "have a great day darlin' I need to roll"

Jim ~ "count me in... I'm here ♥"

Candy ~ ♥ *:)~~*

Sometimes, all it took was to read Candy's comments of her talking to us and with herself to know she was a funny woman. I read this comment about the weird sandwich combo, and all I could think about was the cravings of a pregnant lady. So, I throw my two cents worth into the conversation. I still laugh ever time I read it. This was what was happening online:

Candy ~ *"Gosh I'm hungry .. sudden strange craving for a banana, and peanut butter sandwich ... gosh I hope we have pickles!! yummm"*

Lori ~ likes this.

Candy ~ *"and pistachios yum yum yum"*

Candy ~ *"should go good with cheesecake ..:)"*

Jim ~ "EPT = eat pickles today?"

Candy ~ *"lmao ....ummm could be ??"*

Candy ~ *"need mint chocolate chip ice cream ... yumm"*

Candy ~ *"Ok. you know who.... (pssst ... stand by I'll have the test result in a few minutes!)"*

Candy ~ *"I've got 'em but I'm not sayin' ....omg omg omg...."*
Candy ~ *"ok the answer is ...."*

Candy ~ *"sorry we are experiencing technical difficulties... please stand by...."*

Candy ~ *"still trying to focus on the results...."*

Candy ~ *"the results are in and the answer is... POSITIVELY!..."*

Candy ~ *"NEGATIVE.... ok you can breathe now! :) lol"*

Another evening while Candy was at Bex's house in Georgia I was talking to Candy on the computer. Candy would stop talking when Bex came into the room. Bex would ask her what she was doing and Candy replied:

"none of your business, go downstairs". We would talk a little and Bex would peek back in. Candy would tell her: *"get out of my room and mind your own business."* Bex joked and told her that she was going tell me that she was talking to some other guy and that I was going to be pissed. Candy just laughed.

A few moments later, I heard something hit the floor. I asked Candy what it was and she says: *"you don't want to know"*. This gets me wanting to know even more. Then I hear Candy tell Bex: *"What do I need this for?"*. I asked her again what it was and she finally tells me: *"It's an EPT (Early Pregnancy Test) box"* and we both laugh. It was a good night hearing her joke around with Bex while talking to me at the same time.

CK - CHEMO KIDS

Candy loved kids and she loved helping others even more. One day, we were texting each other when she was at the park relaxing after her walk. She told me about seeing a little girl who was upset because another child took her hat. The little girl had cancer as well and was bald from her treatments. Candy told me she just walked up to her, kneeled down and told the little girl not to worry, that she had the same hair style. She took off her hat and they both laughed. Candy talked to the girl's mom and then continued talking with the little girl for a while telling her she hoped to see her again soon.

On June 4th Candy changes her status: *"is going to the park this morning to meet my new little friend Katie and her friends, with a box full of all kinds of silly and cute hats. Katie and her friends are all "chemo kids". The other kids at the park have been taking their hats from them, so I am going "armed and ready" this morning for a little while! :) Little angels need an extra "halo" now and then. xo*

Lisa ~ "what a wonderful thing to do darl hope u have lots of fun with the kids"

William ~ "That's so awesome of you, Candy.. I hope you have a wonderful time with all of them. God bless you sweetie...."

Candy ~ *"God has blessed me I have wonderful friends like you to keep my spirits up. They loved the hats and the bubbles and ice cream I brought.. It's been a great day!"*

Candy loved helping others even when she wasn't feeling close to 100%. In part of an e-mail she sent me titled "Re: xo" she tells me about motivating herself to get up and going for the kids.

"Trying to talk myself into trudging down the stairs and make all those pancakes and sausage for the CK's as they call themselves this morning. I adore them, but 24 children this morning omg... plus all the parents and chaperones. Bex is setting up tables and chairs in the back yard... Just gotta get through this with a smile on my face it's worth the effort. I'm just not myself today. Can't let them see that. So on will go the goofy hat and smile and I'll try to make it a good morning for them. After that ...I'm heading back to the beach with you! :) Have a safe trip and enjoy yourself. Talk to you soon. No worries ...only love ! xo"

Just over a week later on June 16th, Candy posts about the loss of two of the "CK - Chemo Kids".

Candy ~ *"Is missing someone who they have lost for ever. I wish I could have one more day with you, one more chat one more hug. Rest well little ones... I will never forget your smiles and hugs... R.I.P. ~ Katie & Daniel... just 2 of my C.K.'s that left us this week ...just got the call... my heart breaks. I love you angels xo"*

Lisa ~ "sorry to this candy so sad"

Candy ~ *"♥ 2 of my kids that went to St. Judes last Thursday ... we had a pancake breakfast on Tuesday before they left . I'll never forget my babies xo"*

William ~ "Awwww.. I'm so sorry to hear this Angel... My heart is sad. May the angels pave the streets with streamers of gold and joy as they are welcomed home..."

CHAPTER 6

MOTHER'S DAY

I imagine Mother's Day had to be a hard day for someone whose mother had already passed on, and lost a child of her own. Candy's mother was of Italian descent (*"Mom's family was from Sicily..dont know that I spelled that correctly. I have a bit of a brain fog and can't remember much but I remember that. How? I don't know. Dad's side was Scottish/ Irish too... somewhere in the mix there was Creek Indian.. guess I'm just a buffet of humanity! lol"*) and an independent woman as well. She raised Candy after leaving Candy's father at a young age.

Candy's mother told her that her father had died. I am not sure why she left him but I think it had a little to do with the way he treated people, but you will read more about that later. On this Mother's Day, Candy went to Home Depot and bought weeping cherry trees to plant in remembrance of her and Jimmy's mothers. She said her mother would love seeing these trees swaying in the wind around the lake where Candy once lived.

One thing I will always remember about Candy is that even through her own struggles she would always spread the love online. She didn't want others to worry about her, and would say: *"it will be ok, I will put on my big girl panties to get through it."*

May 9th Candy states: *"Enjoy today as much as possible. Love those you care about with everything in you. Show kindness and compassion to those who just need a little understanding. Give of yourself expecting nothing in return. Experience those things you have waited to try. Hug your children. Love your family and friends without any limitations. Enjoy your life today. It can all be taken away in the blink of an eye..."*

Candy is commenting on her own comments:

"Excuse me while I preach to myself... xo"

"Please let me clarify what I said earlier... HAPPY MOTHER'S DAY TO ALL THE MOTHERS AND TO ALL THE FATHERS WHO HAVE TO BE MOTHER'S TOO! I hope you have a wonderful day!"

"Special (((((HUGS)))) to all the Daddies who have to be mommies too! xo"

Candy's spirit comes out in her words on July 16th: *"At times I may be fragile, but I cannot be broken, simply because I have someone in my life that has my back at all times. ... soooo... heartless idiots beware!"* I hope I was one of the people who had her back like Rae did.

Candy ~ *"You are my friends. When I tell you I love you I mean it. So if it's ever the last time you hear from me ...I hope you know that someone loves you. No one should ever feel unloved. Just know it's the truth. I LOVE YOU .... enough said. xo"*

CHAPTER 7

ESCAPE FROM REALITY

One of Candy's escapes from reality was at the lake. She must had been loved by many of the people who lived there. She would cook food for them, go fishing with them, and just hang out and talk. I don't know who she lived there with, or if she just visited friends who lived around it. You could hear the smile in her voice when we talked about it and the crazy (good) people who were there.

I'm sure she had mixed emotions about the lake after the night that she so wanted to forget. She didn't even want go to sleep at night because, as she told me, the nightmares would come and never leave her alone.

OUR BEACH

Today, I am sitting once again at the beach writing and thinking about Candy. I enjoy seeing kids running after the seagulls, people having their pictures taken wearing white shirts and jeans, and as a friend's father used to say: "people lying in the dirt".

On May 12th, I posted beach pictures on Facebook

because I thought it would make my new friend smile and help out in some way. At that time I didn't know how much Candy loved being at the beach.

There is something comforting about the beach. The sounds of the waves crashing, the seagulls flying, the dolphins swimming, or just sitting collecting your thoughts, it all makes it a great place to be. Candy said: *"I love the beach. The sound, the smell and the feel."* She would walk to the pier down the street from the condo to "people watch" and to see what the fishermen were catching. She enjoyed describing to me the crazy outfits being worn by the tourists. Also, she always said that she wanted her butt planted in the sand for a while. That made me smile.

OUR BEACH PHOTOS 2

After that, I kept posting photos for Candy and we continued talking about how the beach was a great place to relax and clear your head. We both agree that if we only had one place to live, it would be at the beach. Shortly after some of these conversations we started calling the beach *"Our Beach"*. I would tell her that I would love the chance to walk down the beach at sunset with her, holding her hand. She said it would be nice, but since she was now living in Georgia, she didn't know how it could happen. I knew that it might never happen, but I liked her to dream as much as she needed to get her mind off the real world. We would talk about the perfect night on the town and it always began on the beach at sunset, maybe seafood to eat, a glass of wine, and just enjoy each other's company.

Candy ~ *"thank you .. the next best thing to being there. You sure know how to put a smile on my face today. Thanks so much I needed that. xo"*

Jim ~ "my pleasure... have a great day!"

Rae ~ "Thank you for bringing our friend a smile always! ;)"

At this point Candy misses the beach she loves so much. She tells me that Bex has printed the Facebook pictures I took for her and posted them on the walls in her room. Her following comments are about wanting to take a trip, and at the same time, wanting to get her courage up to come see me. Well, at least I hope that is what I was reading into it.

JUNE 15TH

Candy ~ *"Do I want to go to Panama City or Destin????
I need some beach time!!"*

Lisa ~ "Not fair !!!!!"

Lisa ~ "Clean the fridge or wax the floors, decisions, decisions"

Candy ~ *"I don't know if I'm trying to be brave or if I finished losing my mind but I sure do miss it : (."*

Jim ~ "just flip a coin... I win :) either way... lol"

Candy ~ *"you may rethink that !"*

Lisa ~ "I was supposed to get married and run off to Destin some time back, never been there. Oh well, We haven't spoken for a month, Probably for the best.. 24 years of him was enough,,,. lmao"

Candy ~ *"You'd love Destin it's beautiful ... I drove there a few times when I first found out all this was going on with me. Went once and fell asleep on the beach... not peaceful at all lol"*

Lisa ~ "This was years ago, But he last reminded me a couple of months ago, Maybe I should have then... Nah !!!"

Candy ~ *"I promise you ... if nothing else you'll fall in love with the beach there ...and the people are pretty great too!"*

Lisa ~ "I love all beaches, I'm at peace when I get back to them and out of this freaking desert.......I'm a water baby, How I ended up here is beyond me.."

Candy ~ *"Thanks to a certain sweetie, I have the beach surrounding me in my room... would just love to plant my ass in the sand and my toes in the water one more time ..."*

Lisa ~ "Then just do it gf...."

Candy ~ *"Gotta get myself together don't need to go and have days like I had last week. I want to enjoy it.. don't need to go and fall apart there ..who would pick up my pieces? lol"*

Candy ~ *"going back when I die anyway ... scattered on the water, just the way I need to be :)."*

Lisa ~ "That's where my hubby and girls are, and that's where I'll be."

Lisa ~ "I scattered my Bitsy everywhere from santa Cruz Ca, to Hawaii, to the Caribbean, She did love the water..."

Candy ~ *"how sweet"*

Rae ~ "C~ checked on the tix We'll talk ..can't get you on

the phone. Destin or PC either way I'll pick ya up ..just let me know when I'll make the arrangements xo call me puhleeezzz"

Candy ~ *"ok later"*

JUNE 19th

Candy ~ *"My beach was beautiful at 5 a.m. still is , will always be . ~~ Thank you for bringing me back xo i love you xo* ♥♥♥♥♥♥♥ *."*

After returning to Panama City Beach, Candy sends me an e-mail on July 25th titled Re: Hoping your weekend is wonderful. *"Grace and Geo are taking me to sit on the beach for a while today. I will cherish every moment of it as I think of you there with me. Thank you for giving it to me again and again when I couldn't be here. You are always with me in my heart. I love you. Just wanted you to know this today."*

Candy was too weak to walk to the beach herself this day, but still wanted to feel the sun and the sand. She had said that when she passed, she wanted half of her remains to be sprinkled on the beach and half at the lake. She didn't wanted to burden Rae or me with this task. She told us she had asked Pops to do it for her, and I hope he did.

Candy didn't want us to be sad when we went to the beach after she had passed on. She told me: *"I will be the butterfly who shows up unannounced to bring a smile on fluttering wings."* As I was writing this, a butterfly flew by believe it or not, but no tears here, I am smiling.

Candy writes in her journal: *"I tell him I'm ok. He says he wants me to be better than ok. He takes me to the beach again and again. Now it's our beach. God I miss it but he brings me home to it every day."*

OTHER ESCAPES
Downtown Disney and Epcot

In June, I went to Orlando to hangout with some ad fed friends, and to go Epcot prior to attending an advertising conference. I drove down the night before the others were scheduled to arrive. I did this so I could rest before spending the entire next day at Epcot.

I decided a few days before that this was going to be a "Candy trip". I told her we were going to Epcot and that I hoped she enjoyed sharing a room with me, even though I snore. She laughed. When I arrived, I did what I usually do. I went to Downtown Disney to relax and get some dinner. I thought this would be a fun way to start my "jim-n-i"

photos early, and also take some photos just for Candy. The "jim-n-i" are pictures I take with me on the right side and another person on the left. I ask the person I want in the photo with me, who I do not know, if they have gotten their "jim-n-i" photo yet. And they say one of a few things: They say "no", "what is it?", or "no, I am a Taurus not a Gemini". All these answers work for me. I ask them to look here and I hold up my camera, by the time they look up, the picture is already taken. I started doing this as an ice breaker while attending advertising conferences to meet new people, because I am really shy.

I started taking pictures of me and the Disney characters, followed by ones with anybody who would let me, including staff and visitors. Some people asked me why I was doing it, and I would tell them about my friend. Others, just smile and told their friends to come get their picture taken with "this guy". I enjoyed doing the "jim-n-i's" and I also took more pictures of places and things.

I made Candy's name in Legos at the Lego store, saw a coffee mug with her name on it and took a photo of it,

"hope you had one for me too!"

and made a toast with total strangers with a glass champagne. All fun stuff, after that evening and the next day, I had taken over fifty pictures of me and someone for her to laugh at and hopefully enjoy.

See Candy's comments under these photos.

"hey its me! lol"

"beautiful "

"excuse me… is this heaven?"

"ohhhh im so there! lol"

"hey now!"

"too funny"

"Clark Kent in his phone booth! "

CHAPTER 8

VIDEO CHATS - BROADCASTING

Those of you who know me know I love technology. Sure, it's a nerdy statement but who cares? I don't. People have seen me eating lunch or dinner at Panera Bread talking a mile a minute through my computer. They have given me strange looks, even came up to me and asked me what I was doing. I have even broadcast live video at the sports bar "Quig's" just for fun. I would introduce viewers to servers and to other people watching sporting events. Viewers would type in questions and I would answer them. Some of the questions were a little strange, but still fun.

Candy got to experience some of this "fun" as well. One evening when she was watching me talk to her, I asked if she wanted a tour of the sports bar. She said: (typed) *"sure, do it"*. I picked up my laptop and started walking. I walked past the bar, back into the game room and through the dining room back to my "office" booth in the back. Along the way, I told a few people to say hi to Candy and they waved at the camera. Candy said that I was crazy to do this, but whatever. I think she smiled, and I know she typed *"ha ha ha"* in the chat area so it was all good.

The Monday evening before Candy passed away on

Thursday, I asked Candy if she wanted to see me online. I didn't realize this would be the last time I got to talk to her, and for her to hear my voice and see me. I think I acted a fool for over an hour talking about nothing, trying to make her smile, just hanging out as friends. Candy said she wanted to try to get some sleep, and that she would check in with me in the morning.

Before I left, I decided to edit a small piece of the broadcast and e-mail it to her. It was close to the end of the broadcast. I was looking straight into the camera telling her not to worry, that she was not going anywhere. Both of us knew that it was not true. I told Candy she wasn't going anywhere, and that she was always going to be "right here" and pointed at my heart.

http://www.youtube.com/watch?v=u4voZ3Ea2GM

Just me saying good night to you.
Love you . . .

We had always told each other that we would never say good bye, and this was another one of those moments. I e-mailed the broadcast to her and the next morning I checked online to see if she was online. She was on way earlier than I was. I said: "good morning beautiful" in the chat area and she quickly responded: *"hey"*. After talking for a little bit, Candy told me not to think she was crazy and I said: "too late now" followed by: "why should I?". Then Candy said: *"I've already been watching you"*. I didn't know what she was talking about. Then, she reminded me and said she watched my silly video seven or eight times this morning. I jokingly replied: "the hour long show?" followed by: "ha ha ha" and "lol".

She said she watched the whole show once earlier, and the short one seven or eight times. I told her she must have

be really bored to watch a funny looking guy that many times. She replied: *"don't make me come over there and kick your ass"*. I said: "yes ma'am" and then we talked more for a little while until I went to work.

Candy told me this in her journal: *"Monday night was the sweetest night of my life. It was love. It was music. It was you. It was smiles. Laughter. Kisses. And more love. It was you letting me know you would keep me in your heart. I laughed. I cried. I never wanted to leave. I never thought for one moment I could feel so much love. My heart over-flows. And I watched it over again 4 more times just so I could see your face, hear your voice. This thing is crazy. It's unexplainable. It's nothing I was looking for but something that found me and completely took me by surprise."*

And yes, my eyes still water up every time I read this one. It was me having fun still knowing it wouldn't last much longer.

CHAPTER 9

PHONE CALLS & VOICEMAILS

It's funny how you can get to know people by just texting and talking on the phone. While working in one of my "satellite" offices, as I call them, (anywhere with free wireless) I would check in on my friend Candy, to see how her day was going. Some days of course were better than others. But the times I enjoyed most were when I could get on Yahoo! Messenger and talk to Candy and hear her voice. These days you could find out very fast if it was a good day or not. Most of the times when I asked her if she wanted to talk were good days. Her "Southern" accent was as good as they get and wow!, that sense of humor was too much. We would talk about general stuff like the weather, what was going on outside her window, where I was sitting working today, or what I was working on.

I remember hearing her smoke alarm in the condo chirping like it needed its battery to be replaced. Candy said they changed it but it didn't help, so she learned to tune it out. She told me I had a built-in *"Candy BS Detector"* and that it was always on. She couldn't or better not even try to lie 'cause I would know the truth or at least she thought I did. I think that, once you get to know your friends, you know when they are in a good or bad mood and if you should talk or just leave them alone.

We would talk for as long as Candy could before wanting to rest or get something to eat. Sometimes, I would talk to her while working or we would just hang out not saying anything. We would be connected; she would be looking around on the internet, listening to music, say something every now and then, and I would be close by. I can't imagine how hard it was for her to sleep knowing how little time she had left on this earth.

When dealing with her pain, Candy would say: *"I wish somebody would just shoot me"* because it was so intense. I told her just to scream. She would reply that the people in the next rooms of the condo would think something was going on. With that in mind, me being the crazy guy I am, I told her: "well, scream my name and see what happens." She laughed and said: *"Pops would be in here looking for the man"*. One message I received in June said this: *"of course I screamed your name all night! doesn't mean it was always in pain ... :) "*. It made me smile.

Most of the times that I got to talk with Candy were through my computer. I did ask her to call and leave me a message if she was awake late at night and those are here.

I received three voicemails from Candy during our

brief relationship. The first was: *"Well, I didn't want you to go another day without hearing my lovely voice, ha ha ha - isn't that a joke. I'll catch you later, um yeah, I'll catch you later. Have a good day. Bye now."* This is a small sample of the fun personality I enjoyed everyday. The day after Candy passed, I posted this voicemail on her Facebook page so her other friends could hear her voice whenever they wanted to.

A few days later she left me a second voicemail, where Candy being Candy says: *"Hello, You have been enrolled in the "obscene phone call of the month", ok so maybe not. Anyway, looks like I was right, ummm it looks like I'll be out of here by the end of the week. I'll talk to you later have a good evening. Bye."* This is more of Candy playing around even through her tough times before moving to Georgia with Bex.

The hardest one for me to listen to was, and is, the last voicemail I received from her. It was two days before she lost her battle against cancer. Her voice was shaking, sounded even a little bit scared, and I could hear her heart talking to me. Damn those tears again! She would always say that she had cried enough for everyone already and not to waste mine. Oh well, time to listen again to get it right here. The last voicemail is almost two minutes long (she paused a few times in-between words). Candy says:

"Hi Jim, I just wanted to tell you… I am… I love you, and… ummm you take care of yourself okay? Thank you for always, always being here… you'll never, never know how much it has meant to me. I've not been well. Now I know what love feels like. I just wanted to say thank you. Wherever I go, you go with me. And, I'll see you on the beach ok? I love you, always will. Take care of yourself ok? ok? I'll see you one day. Just don't you be in a hurry to see me ok? You have a lot to do, a lot of people to make smile. You sure made me smile and I thank you. I love you, take care. ok? You're in my heart." It is so hard to listen to Candy's voice knowing she is gone. In the first line, where Candy says: *"I am…"* and pauses, is where she would tell me that she was sorry for putting me through all of this. I would tell her not to tell me she was sorry, but to tell me "to go *#@% off" or to tell me "I love you". She would say that she would never tell me the first one, I am glad I got to hear her tell me she loved me in her last voicemail.

All I know, is that I need to keep on doing whatever it is I do to make people smile, because Candy wants me to.

CHAPTER 10

THE MUSIC & VIDEOS

Music is one of those things in life I can not live without. I wake up to it, and sometimes go to sleep with it still playing. It soothes my soul, relaxes me, makes me dance, and even makes me smile. Candy and I had this in common. Candy said: *"My choices of music have always been odd to most. But I've always loved music. It's brave enough to say what you can't. The window to your soul mom always said. But you know this already you get it. How can people get through their lives without music?"*

From time to time we both would post music videos reflecting our moods or as subtle messages to the people in our lives. Candy's music tastes were all over the place, in a good way. When she was having a rough day she would post something to help pick herself up. If she was feeling *"frisky"*, under the influence of her medications, or *"truth serum"* as she put it, she would post something more risqué. Also, she would have a little comment to introduce the song choice to start the discussions.

I would use music to motivate Candy in little videos I post online. Candy was not enjoying the effects of the chemo treatments and would get down mentally, who wouldn't? The first video I did on May 26th was called: "Candy's Beach" and it had both video and stills with jazz music from the Braxton Brothers playing in the background. I used text on top of the video to say comforting and encouraging words: "Candy's Beach", "catching rays...", "relax with me...", "puffy clouds...", "skim boarding...", "good times...", "for all my good friends", "smile more...", and "hug someone...".

Sometimes, she would tell me she wished she wasn't fighting anymore and was done. What could I say to this? I am not a psychiatrist and it scared me. I remember telling her to hold on because she is here for a reason, even if we didn't know what that reason was.

The second video I posted was: "Hold On" with music by Tyrone Wells. A little two minute video with footage from the aquarium, the beach, and fireworks from 4th of July videos I had taken last year. It was June 20th and my comment read: "just a little eye candy for a friend. hope she likes it & thank you tyrone wells for great music as always...". Tyrone Wells sings: "Hold on, Hold on to me, Hold me close and hold me near, Breathe assurance in my ear, Hold on..." and I know his words help comfort Candy.

The third video was: "By Your Side" with music by Sade. It had beach photos that I had taken for her, and others I had taken in the past. We both knew, or felt, that Candy's time on earth was not going to be long. I wanted her to know that I was not going anywhere, not going to leave her alone. I was going to be here for her as long as she wanted me. Some of Sade's touching lyrics were: "You think I'd leave your side baby? You know me better than that. You think I'd leave down when you're down on your knees? I wouldn't do that..."

This was around the same time of the oil spill and my comment on the video read: "Whether it's being there for a friend or protecting our beautiful beaches everyone needs to help out and do what we can do."

Shortly after Candy decided to fight her battle a little more, we found a couple more reasons why she was still here on earth. At the condo, a young man collapsed outside by the pool. Candy performed CPR on him until the fire station guys got there to assist, and take him to the hospital. If that was not enough, a week or so after this incident, one of Pop's friends had a heart attack at the condo. Candy had to *"climb him"*, as she said, to give him CPR. He was a very tall gentleman and I believe he was thankful she was there for him. After this, the condo employees were given CPR training, and it became a requirement for employment.

MUSIC VIDEOS

After talking for a couple of months we had gotten to know each other well. I was still wanting to meet her in person and hang out together. On July 1st, I posted a link to a Rascal Flatts video. In their lyrics they say: "I wanna know everything about you... where your hopes and dreams and wishes live", and that's how I felt too. Candy said she couldn't or didn't want to look into the eyes of someone she cared for, and have to tell them goodbye or hurt them.

Jim Clark ~ "just saying . . ."

Rascal Flatts - "Take Me There" - Official Video

Rae ~ likes this.

Candy ~ *"It's a rough and rocky road... better traveled with a true friend. xo"*

Jim ~ "take me there . . . xOxOxOx"

Candy ~ *"you pop the popcorn ... I've got the tickets! xoxoxoxo"*

The posting of music videos was something we both enjoyed doing. Some of Candy's favorite groups and songs are listed here. I think you can tell a lot about a someone's personality by their music tastes. Also, you can tell what kind of mood they are in, and if you listen hard enough, you may even hear some words that are meant for you.

Tyrone Wells "More" and "Need"
Jill Scott "A Long Walk" and "He Loves Me"
Rascal Flatts "Everyday" and "Take Me There"
Charlotte Church "Call My Name"

Uncle Kracker "Smile"
Beauty and The Bass "Makin Whoopee"
Luther Vandross "Never Too Much"
Andrea Bocelli "Cant Help Falling In Love"
Alicia Keys "No One" and "If I Ain't Got You"
Sarah McLachian "I Will Remember You"
Darius Rucker "Alright"

These are only just a few of the artists and songs she enjoyed. She had many more and said this about it: *"My choices of music have always been odd to most. But I've always loved music. It's brave enough to say what you can't. The window to your soul mom always said. But you know this already you get it. How can people get through their lives without music? I've wanted to go back through the links I've used and write them down. But I haven't. Guess I've just been lazy that way. I think by now you know how I feel. You know where to find it all.*

Jim dear you are my music. Are you smiling?

You'd better be!"

CHAPTER 11

AD3 - TATTOO

AD3 was created to get people with similar beliefs together; to have fun and take care of each other while doing it. I started this group back in 1992 while attending advertising conferences. The conferences were fun but becoming full of drama. Too much of the "we are bigger, so we are better" mentality or maybe just power hungry driven people looking for the spotlight, I don't know. I just knew I wanted to change something about my experience while attending these conferences.

Within the organization (American Advertising Federation - District 4) there are regular Advertising Federation members and AD2 members. The AD2 members are advertising professionals 32 years old and younger. I, for some reason, hang out with the younger members. I guess because they would still go out dancing and exploring the local sights instead of just hanging out at the hotel. We would go to clubs, dance, and have a cocktail or two. If the ladies in our group were getting "hit on" by people they didn't want to talk to, we would act as if we were married. This would end the conflicts most of the time. And, if any of the people in our group had too much to drink, (like Lisa, Megan, and that other girl from the Nashville conference) we would make sure they got back to the hotel safely.

Well, by now you are wanting to know why I am telling you about this organization. I did it because Candy became a member. And before I forget, our logo is ". . ." an ellipses. We say it's what happens when the meeting agenda ends at 6 p.m. and before the next agenda begins early the next day.

How did Candy become a member without even attending a meeting? Well, it's like this, a few of us have the ". . ." logo tattooed on our bodies. I decided to be the first one a few years back followed by others. There were a total of 11 members with tattoos, but having it is not a requirement for membership. On June 15th, Candy decided to be #12.

I was attending a conference when I saw the photo used as her profile picture. Candy had added "Hold On" and ". . ." to her existing butterfly tattoo. I didn't think it was real, so I text her: "Is this for real?" followed by: "smilin'". I didn't really know what to say. I took my computer and showed it to my fellow AdFed/AD3 members Jessi, Elizabeth, and Mara, and told them what happened. Let's just say it was a great AD3 moment for me.

What was she thinking? Well, when I go back to her journal I see this: *"Hold on, Hold onto me... I love this song too. That's it! I'll keep my Jim with me at all times. I'll do it tomorrow. I'll add Hold On . . . to my tattoo. A reminder on my worst of days right there to remind me I'm never alone. I'm just crazy enough to do it. I need the reminder. Damn now he'll be showering with me too! Makes me smile, but he may think I'm insane. Won't be the first time a man has thought that. Probably won't be the last. Did it! Tattooed the tit!"*

I still smile every time I read that. And when I look at my AD3 tattoo, which is on my right wrist, I think of my group of friends. Most of them are still here on earth, but a few have passed on. I think of her. I remember when Candy wrote: *"Some days 3 little dots . . . just make my day"* and I agree.

CHAPTER 12

FAMILY

Growing up without a father around has got to be rough. I don't know how single moms do it, raising a child or children on their own. Candy's mother told Candy that her father had died when she was very young. I know that on Father's Day she thought about what it would have been like if he was around. If he would have been there by her side through the treatments comforting her. Candy, knowing that the chemo was not working and she was not going to be around anymore, decided to see if she had any family. Candy got her lawyers to hire a private investigator to do the research.

Sometime around the end of June Candy got a response. She writes: *"Today Pops brought me a letter from the lawyers. My father is alive and well. An executive at a large corporation. His letter has a check for $25,000 in it. All I have to do is never contact him he says mom and I ruined his life. He tells me, his daughter that I am vomit from his past. I need to be washed away from his memory to take the money and leave him alone. What the fuck? I didn't know he existed. How the hell did I ruin his life? He has lived well while mom and I struggled to keep food in the house, a roof over our heads and lights on."*

photo collages in this chapter were created with pictures from my family albums

I think - how in the world can somebody be so cold hearted? He didn't want to know how she was, if she was married, did she have children, or anything a normal caring parent would want to know first. He tells her that she is: "the vomit from his past" and now I want to meet this ass and give him a piece of my mind. Sorry, I had a moment and it made me feel sick as well. I could only think of my kids and what they would think if I was acting that way. Shame on him to offer her money so she would stay out of his life and leave him alone. I don't know why Candy's mother told her that he had died, but if this was a sample of his personality and how he treated people, I definitely understand.

Candy continues to write and I can feel her rage: *"I feel something I've not felt it's hate and I don't like it. Disgust. He makes me want to vomit and I do. I'm really sick now. He never once made an effort to contact me. The lawyers hired a private investigator to find any family I might have. I wish he had stayed dead. I am nothing to him and he makes me feel less than nothing. Fuck him and his money."*

I talked to her about this and she is hurt and mad. I tried to get her to calm down but it's not working tonight. Instead, she decides she is going to drink and start a fire. I worry the fire is going to be in her room at the condo, but she assures me that she has a little grill outside that will work for what she wants to do. She tells me and also writes: *"Let's get drunk and burn this mother fucker."* I try to get her to sleep on it and come back to it in the morning, but she tells me it's too late. She burns the check and his letter and says: *"I watch the check and his letter burn, it feels good. I'm not for sale."* We talked for a little bit longer, she told me to go get some rest, that she will be in a better mood tomorrow.

ANOTHER DAY

After talking with the doctor, he suggested that she tries the chemo treatment again. She has put on a little bit of weight, and her energy level is much stronger. In this e-mail, she talks about preparing to start chemo again and how she wants her life back. The e-mail continues with her step sisters and brothers wanting to get to know her, and a little love for me.

E-mail "on the road again..." June 27th:

Stocked the freezer with popsicles & ice cream. Stocked up on gatorade, pedialyte, soup & crackers. I won't say I'm ready to start chemo again, but I'm preparing. Soooo not looking forward for the torture to begin again. But there's a chance it could help, who knows? I've got nothing else

to do anyway right? It's not like I'm doing anything impor-
tant . Just surviving. Tired of just surviving. I want my life
back. But since that's not going to happen, I'll take the best
I can get. Not many choices left for me.

This thing with sisters and brothers wanting to get to
know me, it's nuts right? I'm the big sister with all the
issues. Nothing worth knowing and I certainly don't need
to dump all of this in their lap. I'm sure they are amazing
people. 2 sisters with a catering biz. 3 brothers an engi-
neer, a nurse and one in college working on a degree in ad-
vertising. twin brothers ...good thing I wasn't a twin! It's a
lot to digest. Don't know if I will make the call just yet. But
I won't ignore them like I've been ignored either. I refuse
to degrade myself to their father's level. Their mother told
them about me she opened the letter from the attorney. Mr.
Wonderful certainly didn't tell them. Too much happening
right now. I'll figure it out one step at a time. No worries.
Sorry this is so long today. A lot on my mind.

Hope your trip was wonderful. Come home safely so I
can torture you again! :) ... thanks for being my sounding
board. I know it's not always easy. I do appreciate you, I
hope you know that.

I love ya Jim ~~ xxxooo ~~ Candy

MORE NEWS

In her journal Candy writes: *"Another letter today from the attorneys much like came before but this one comes with dread. What more could it be right? I'm so sick today I can't keep anything down. I feel weak. Don't need anymore surprises but it's probably nothing. Breathe Candy just breathe. That's what Jim would say. Nothing could top the last letter anyway. Ok maybe I'm not ready yet. Try to sip on a shake and pull myself together, then open it."*

"These are my siblings. Just when I thought there could be no more surprises. Boom! Here we go. My dead father has 5 more children. His wife didn't know I existed until she intercepted the attorneys letter. She then told the children who now want to know their big sister. WTF? This is too much, I'm so overwhelmed I don't know how to feel. I hate him more. I don't like this feeling. I can't sink to his level."

She also writes about meeting her step family saying: *"It's not their fault. How can I introduce myself to them? I'm dying, I feel it everyday. I try to push it aside but it eats away at me every day. How can I say hello to them, get to know them and tell them ok the jokes on you 'cause I'm dying. Goodbye. How cruel is all of this?"*

June 29th

Candy ~ *"Received a package at 6 am from family I never knew I had. Haven't opened it just yet. Wondering, will it explode? Will I find good things or will it just be one more thing to blow up in my face? I just sit here staring at this box. Do I open it or toss it? I don't need one more thing to slap me in the face. I've had enough of that. I think I'll just wait a while, sit, smile & eat more ice cream."*

Candy ~ *"I am so glad I have wonderful friends who have become my family. No matter what happens, I know they will always be here for me. xo"*

I told Candy she just needed to let someone she trusts open her mail and packages. I told her to get Rae or Pops to do it if they were there. Then, she wouldn't have to deal with stressful things and not even worry about it.

July 1st, Candy continues to vent online about the letter and check from her father:

Candy ~ *"I'd rather go for a walk on the beach in the rain and wait for my rainbow, than count $ in the bank to help a cold hearted, uncaring, selfish fool feel better about himself. I am so much better than that. What's left of my heart is worth more than the fool and his money could ever afford. I am content where I am and I am rich in friends who love me."*

Candy ~ *"I need nothing more than more time to show those who love me how much they are loved in return. No amount of money can buy that. No matter what it may look like I know I am blessed."*

Later that day, Rae is there to offer some support and Candy let's her know she will be ok:

Rae ~ "There's always time to fall. But real strength is shown when you Stand in spite of falling down. Get up girl. Shake it off. There are people in our lives that will never change. Just breathe, chin up, shoulders back, Stand tall and proud of the person you are. YOU are stronger than you think. Braver than most. And you are ABOVE one person's guilt. Let him carry that load. It's NOT YOUR BURDEN TO BEAR! ...Just breathe, and love with all your heart. Just be!"

Rae ~ "you are never alone. you are loved. No one can take that from you!"

Candy ~ *"I've got my team J&R to back me up ... I'll be ok no worries I love you. He might have stomped on my heart, but he can't destroy what was already in it. xo"*

CHAPTER 13

FINAL DAYS

Candy and I are now talking about Italy and speaking Italian. Grace, the lady who lives next door, teaches her a couple of words and we begin to play "Italian Style". I opened up an Italian translation program on my computer and changed words from English to Italian and text them to Candy. Before you know it, we are saying all kinds of crazy stuff. The ones that will stay with me are: *"Io vi amo per sempre"* meaning "I will love you forever" and *"ti amo molto"* that means "I love you very much."

"Sempre e persempre"

Candy writes hers in the journal: *"Io non sara mai lasciare solo voi mi sono con voi sempre . . . Too late we try Italian but it was fun with you today. You already know this xo Always and Forever"* It translates to read *"I will not ever leave you alone I am with you always"*

Candy would have rough days coping with the pain she was feeling in her head due to the tumor. Whenever she was in pain or having trouble breathing she would use music to comfort herself. She would also encourage others to have a good weekend, and told us to enjoy every minute of our day, knowing that time can be short.

July 17th

Candy ~ *"I truly have sweet fbook friends. No worries... I'm ok.. spending the weekend being serenaded by Tyrone, Luther & Andrea... with J.C. waiting for a whisper if I need anything... (both of them I'm sure :)) It's all good. Enjoy your weekend. No worries... only love. Enjoy every minute of your day today. I love you. xo"*

July 18th she shares the love and encourages people to *"love someone while you have the chance."*

Candy ~ *"When all is said and done... how will you re-member me? Will you throw up your hands in the air and say "Candy who?" or "She finally shut up!" lol... I hope somewhere along the way you will just quietly remember the silly girl in the goofy hat with the crazy grin and just .... smile ~~~ Have a lovely Sunday. Love someone while you have the chance. xo"*

Candy ~ *"Time is so short... Fill it up with love and laugh-ter. In the end, that's all that really matters. I love you. You are my friend. And that is what friends do ... love love love xo.*

Rae ~ "I will remember you as the most courageous woman I've ever met. Who faced adversity with a smile and determination. A woman who put others needs before her own. A woman who could light up the darkest room just with her presence and her smile. I will remember you as my dearest friend who grabbed my heart and wouldn't let go. you will be with me every day and i will always remember my friend Candy who was as sweet as her name and could make you laugh and smile on your worst day. My friend Candy, a treasure that I hold dear. i love you."

July 24th

Candy ~ *"Letting go of yesterday's pain isn't always easy. If I let my heart be overwhelmed by the hurt of those who don't care, then there is very little room for the love of those who try to reach out today. Time today for some heart cleaning. If it's no good kick it to the curb with the rest of the trash. Fill me up... Your love has healed the brokenness in me and I can go on. xo"*

Karen ~ "How true. Hope you find peace today!"

Sometimes while talking Candy would catch herself complaining about the hurt others had caused her. She would tell me she was sorry, and I would tell her that they didn't care and it was still affecting her, not them. I also told her that she should leave it in the past and live her life the best she could.

In my mind, *"I'm sorry"* was a phrase Candy started using too much. She would tell me: *"I'm sorry for putting you though this"*, *"I'm sorry you have to hear all of this"*, and *"I'm sorry..."*. It made me sad and upset because I didn't want her to dwell on it. I wanted her not to be hurting, worrying, or suffering from anything. Sometimes she would ask: *"why do you put up with it?"* and I would answer her by saying: "I can leave anytime I want to, but I am here until you tell me to leave." I knew I wasn't going anywhere, I was committed and I would be right here to do anything for her.

ACCEPTANCE

July 24th

Candy ~ *"I love... I have been loved ... I am still loved. In the end that's all that matters. Thank you for being by my side. It's been a bumpy ride. This ride's almost over. That's ok. I have peace of mind, love in my heart and a smile on my face. I'm good to go ... and just think... you were a part of making that possible. I'll never forget any of you xo"*

Candy ~ *"Time to rest a while xo have a lovely weekend everyone. xoxoxo"*

July 25th

Candy ~ *"I never say goodbye. But always see ya soon. Please don't send me any goodbye emails now. I've cried enough for all of us in the past few months. Let's just smile. Laugh. Love. I am at peace. I am fine. It's a beautiful day. A friend is taking me to sit on my beach one more time today. I will cherish it as I cherish every thought of you. I love you my friends. It really is ok."*

Candy ~ *"Life is sometimes hard, even painful. But I know where I'm going when I leave here. So goodbye is not an option. I'll be watching over you all. I love you. Enjoy your day. Enjoy your life. It's too short to spend it sad. Smile. Laugh. Play. and above all, LOVE!!!!"*

Rae ~ "You have made my world a more beautiful place to be. I love you."

Mark ~ "Praise the Lord!"

I posted a video when we had been talking about the future. I didn't know what to say. This was my first time talking about death with someone who was so close to me emotionally. I figured, having someone there to hold your hand would be a good start. Then I told her when she leaves this earth, it will not be over, and I want her to save me a seat next to her in heaven.

Jim Clark "the best that I can . . ."
Hootie And The Blowfish - "Hold My Hand" Video

July 25
Candy ~ *"one of my favorites .. thank you xoxoxoxoxoxo"*

Jim ~ "and remember to save me a seat on your left to hold your hand"

Candy ~ *"you got it!"*

Candy knew the end was in sight and writes in her journal: *"My breathing is a little more difficult today. I know it won't be much longer now. But Jim it's really ok. I had a dream again about my baby, my mom and Jazmyn. They are waiting for me. It will be wonderful to hold my little one in my arms. She has always been in my heart. I'm a terrible person you know? I never even dared to dream of giving her a name. So much is missing. But soon I will be complete. You have filled in so much that has been missing from my heart and life."*

I recall one evening while we were talking online, Candy asked me if I would help her do something. Of course my answer was "yes". Then she said: *"no that's okay you have helped me with so much already"* and I thought I haven't help much, so I persisted and said: "let me help, I want to, what is it?" That's when Candy said she wanted to finish doing some things she had not done.

Tonight, it was going to be naming her unborn daughter. Wow! I thought, this is a big one. She told me a couple of names she came up with. I told her they were nice, but they didn't remind me of her, we needed to have a name to reflect "family". So, with that said, I recommended Candace Noelle because Candy's name was in Candace. Candy then tells me that Candace was her grandmother's name. I thought about it, and told her: "perfect", and since Noelle was Candy's middle name, it felt right. She told me: *"thanks for helping I can now cross that one off my list."*

CHAPTER 14

MESSAGES, E-MAILS, & PHOTOS

Being that I only talked to Candy for a few months, I decided to include messages, e-mails, and photos with comments. We communicated quite a bit online; not only by voice, but through posting comments, music videos, and messages. Here are a few with some added comments from me. Ok, maybe more than a few, but I wanted to include these and those in here too.

Candy ~ commented on your photo:
"Thank you Jim ;)"

Followed by an Facebook message. Subject: hi

I sent you an e-mail but thought I would say thank you here also. You made my day. I attempted to send you a text through yahoo chat & mobile text but it did not go through. I probably had the wrong number anyway. I hope you have a lovely weekend . Thanks for the beach I am always amazed at your thoughtfulness. xo ~ Candy

On May 21st, Candy's friend Bex picked up Candy to move just outside of Atlanta so she could take care of her there. This was also the same day I posted "Candy 2" another set of beach photos online. This time was different from the first because I decided to tell people what I was doing, versus just taking pictures. It is very interesting to talk to others about dealing with cancer, and how it affects lots of us. Some people would just say: "that's a nice thing to do" and others would ask: "what kind of cancer?" and "how are the treatments going?". But the nicest things were when I was saying goodbye. They told me they would have Candy in their thoughts and prayers. This was great to hear, since they didn't know her at all, but were still concerned about another person.

On May 23rd, I decided to answer one of Candy's e-mails the way I do sometimes, by saying something in-between the lines. The italic text is Candy's and the bold is mine.

Hi Jim,
Hey Candy...

I am home now here just outside of Atlanta. My friend Rebecca has everything set up for me. My lovely bed with tons of big fluffy pillows just the way I like it. Everything within reach.

The times you get down all you need to do is grab one of you big fluffy pillows and give it/me a hug. A friend

of mine in Florida said it worked for her. lol

I peeked in earlier after Rachel gave me a heads up on the photos. That's about the sweetest thing anyone's done for me. You always made the chemo sessions easier. Just the chatting away and then you took me to the beach. That really touched my heart that you would do that for me. And here you have done it again. It really does help. Bex said if that's what it takes to see me smile again she's printing them all and putting them all around my room! LOL That's fine by me.

It was because of your fun personality that I did it. I love to make people smile! I am a smart ass sometimes but people who put up with me become even better friends.

I just wish I could have gotten well enough to have met you in person. But that is ok because now I have you with me every day. Your photos keep me company.

My brother and his family are moving to somewhere near Atlanta so don't count meeting me in person out yet : P...

I made a lot of mistakes and I've learned from them too little too late. I will probably not allow myself to go on facebook much anymore. I'm just far too embarrassed by things I've done and dont want to hurt anyone further.

Don't worry about the things you have done in the past or even more about what people think about you.

I would still love to hear from you if you dont mind. I promise to respond as much as I am able. Some days I just sit back and watch the monitor to see who is there or if I get new posts. I really did not know how far this illness had taken over I didnt know how sick I was. The chemo just isnt working. But it's ok I have made peace with my life. And right now I have this very moment today and I will enjoy it to the best of my ability.

I will be available to you for as long as you'll have me as your friend.

As long as I can open my eyes, I'm taking a stroll on the beach with you admiring all the incredible things there are to take in. And by the way thanks for the wave and for sticking your toes in the water for me! That was awesome. I'm a little tired right now so I will go. I hope to hear from you again soon. Keep those photos coming. I swear I can hear the sound of the waves and the seagulls flying overhead when I look at them. Thank you for being such a dear sweet friend to me in my hardest times. I'd like to ask a favor of you if you don't mind. Would you please just check in on Rachel for me from time to time if its only to say hello? She took care of me through some very trying times and came running at a moments notice to help me. She is really taking this very hard. To tell her not to worry about me is just silly. She does. She always has since I met her and she probably always will. I think a lot of fbook people have given her a hard time about me. But I promise you Jim I am not a figment of anyones imagination. Today I live and breathe. I would just appreciate it if you could just give her a hello to keep her spirits up it would be really nice.

I said hey to Rae this morning. I will be shooting more pictures because I love doing it and if it makes people happy even better. I have meet many people taking my "Jim-n-I" pictures and have fun in the process

I must go for now. Thank you for everything my sweet friend. I hope you always will remember me and smile. I know that I smile when I think of you. Take care.

Keep smiling and thank you for making me smile too. Take care and I look forward to talking to you again soon.

Your "beach buddy"

That guy in Florida who you just kinda met...
~ Candy ~~ love ya xo

Jim - much love and happiness xOxOxOx

" xOxOxOx" is the AD3 way to send kisses and hugs to friends with the . . . 's in the middle.

Candy ~ May 22, 2010 at 12:42pm

Re: hi

Gotcha! Take care my sweet friend xo

You are simply the best ;) xo

Jim - much love and happiness xOxOxOx

Candy commented on your photo:

"Why do you always have to be so sweet to me?

You've never let me down ... xo"

Candy commented on your photo:

"my hero xo"

ok sweetie xxx I owe you big... going to eat now just for you ... what would I do without you?

This one explains itself. I heard Candy wasn't eating much because she had said it made her nauseous. While a few of us would tell her individually to eat, it took all of us to get her to do it. This day was a success as you can see.

May 26

"And almost an hour later... I did ok . .. so far so good!"

Candy ~ *"Hope you all feel better now... I dood it for you ... no worries now ok? xo"*

Jim ~ "Ok what's for dessert? Or better yet dinner... xOxOxOx"

Candy ~ *"I think I'm gonna bake banana bread for every-one .. I might even try some ..."*

Rae ~ "now that makes me feel so much better thank you Candy honey xo I can rest better now"

Candy ~ *"I hope so .. :)"*

Candy ~ May 29, 2010 at 2:35pm

Re: :)

A very short walk but it was nice. I guess sitting in the park isn't so bad. lol....... A lot of pain today but no worries...it's just a thing I have to deal with. Being a good little girl and drinking my "fat girl" shakes ! lol just thankful for AC again. Sat out on the balcony most of the night just looking at that big orange moon. Came back in around 3am to "walk on the beach" with you.

Life is good. I have my 3 amigos and the rest can fall by the wayside, my fbook list is getting smaller and smaller and I'm ok with that. I just can't let ignorant people get to me anymore. Too much to deal with already without the drama of ignorance.

Wish my butt was planted in the sand today but instead I'll accept the lovely magnolia trees outside surrounding the balcony. It's not my beach but it can be peaceful at times. ok I'll stop rambling.. lol (..yeah right he says) miss talking to you today can you tell? lol Have a lovely weekend ~ :) ♥ ♥ ♥

Candy and I spent the afternoon chatting online and I had joked about picking her up and going out dancing. I told her that she could dance with me and Lindsey, or just go crazy on the dance floor by herself. This was the e-mail I had waiting for me when I returned home later that night.

Candy May 31, 2010 at 12:51am

Subject: Good night xo

Going to try to get some rest. It was so nice to talk to you as always. Have a wonderful Memorial Day. Rest well tonight. Talk to you tomorrow, hopefully. Take care and don't shake it too much with JLo ...lol xo sweet dreams ....

XXXOOOXXX

"Thank you Megan and April..."

"The kids across the way heard I wasn't feeling well and brought me some juice boxes and tootsie pops! Special delivery with hugs included. Just what a crazy girl like me needed today. Their smiles were priceless and they brought me pictures too ...the little budding artists. Just once more proves to me that there is still good in the world even if it is found in the face of a child."

"Look what happened... I woke up again ... and it's weigh in day. Guess what happened?"

Candy ~ *"Someone got his wish!"*

Larry ~ "That's a good posative !!!!!!:)"
          "Very good news!!!"

Larry ~ "My friend was taking Ensure and protein shakes"

Jim ~ "Love it... keep it going ;)"

Candy June 5, 2010 at 9:35am

Subject: Sorry to leave like that last night

Lots of lightning here and then to top it off a fire in the kitchen. So I never made it back on. Never a dull moment at the "Bex Hilton" LOL . Jim I know this sounds crazy (what doesn't coming from me? right?) but I get every- thing sent to Rae's place and she has a friend who is a courier that is here Monday through Friday on her route and she brings me my mail, packages, and what not. Just for the simple fact that Bex's assistants open everything. And yes I mean EVERYTHING without looking to see who it's addressed to. I just choose to not let them open what is mine, and since Rae has it arranged this way for me, believe it or not it's less stressful. Yes I know I'm just a nut case! I just have a network of people helping me. Guess I should feel important by now huh? lol. Anyway anything you choose to send can be sent to me c/o Rae (address). I can assure you I will more than likely get things either the same day they are delivered or the following day. She (Diane) hand delivers them to me. It's a crazy world I live in. (Inside and outside my head LOL). Thanks for under- standing. I enjoyed our chat last night even with my sweet crazy Bex in the mix. She always keeps things interesting anyway! Have a lovely day... hope you get some sand between your toes for me today :) . Take care my dear sweet friend. Talk to you soon xo

~~Candy~~

Candy June 5, 2010 at 12:29pm

Re: Sorry to leave like that last night

I'm lovin it!!! ;) you've got me smiling ... as always!

Candy June 8, 2010 at 8:20am

Re: xo

I finally slept ...about an hour I think? An hour is good considering I had not slept since I fell asleep on the balcony Saturday.

It was nice to have this message when I logged in this morning. But then again, it's always nice to hear from you any time.

I sat up looking at our beach all night, wishing I was there. Sleep just wasn't going to be the "main event" of the night that's for sure. Listened to music and did some writing.

Trying to talk myself into trudging down the stairs and make all those pancakes and sausage for the CK's as they call themselves this morning. I adore them, but 24 children this morning omg... plus all the parents and chaperones. Bex is setting up tables and chairs in the back yard... Just gotta get through this with a smile on my face it's worth the effort. I'm just not myself today. Can't let them see that.

So on will go the goofy hat and smile and I'll try to make it a good morning for them. After that... I'm heading back to the beach with you! :)

Have a safe trip and enjoy yourself. Talk to you soon. No worries ...only love ! xo

Candy June 9, 2010 at 2:03am

Re: xo

Don't need the bail money! Finally saw the doc around 5. She felt so badly about how long I had to wait she had someone drive me home and had my jeep towed home. Whats up with that? Never happened before. Anyhoo, Im safe at home didnt choke the dr. ... now for that drink... What a day ! :) talk to ya soon xo love ya

June 10, 2010 7:24:51

Candy commented on her status:

"skipped the ice cream sorry... but the rest was ok :)"
":) aww thanks..."

Candy commented on her link:

"You'd better like it! lol :)"

"me too! <3<3<3<3<3<3"

Candy June 11, 2010 at 12:15pm
Subject: good morning

Hope your day goes well. Mine's pretty good so far.

The nurse showed up at 6 am to hook me up to the iv. Never thought I'd say this but this morning... morphine is good! The first time in weeks I'm not feeling any pain.

I have a feeling I will be in the naughty chair for a very long time though. Bex says its like truth serum for me . LOL.. she's laughing her ass off at me and I could care less today.

I might actually sleep sometime today.

Good thing you didn't call me this morning you might have heard things you didn't want to hear :) I'll catch up with you later Mr. Hot tub! LOL ... gotta behave myself today before I molest the pool boy! LOL Have a great day xo love ya

Candy commented on her status:
":)~~"

Candy commented on her status:
"woo to the hoo! ;)"

 *My package was delivered a short time after we talked this morning. I can't even begin to tell you how incredibly beautiful it all is. This has been an amazing day. I couldn't ask for more. The painting is amazing Jim. No one has ever done anything like this for me. I've been in tears all day ... good tears mind you. Everything is absolutely perfect. And your mom... how sweet. I am just so grateful for everything.*

There are people that I see all the time that I call my friend. And then there is you, I've never met you face to face, but what an incredibly amazing friend you are to me. You have brought me such joy. You've gotten me through some of the most painful days. I just don't think I would have survived this long without your kindness and support.

Saying thank you is so inadequate. So very small in comparison to what you have given me. But I do thank you and I am grateful and blessed to have you in my life.

I love you Jim. xo
~~ Candy xo

*"signs of a crazy lady...
heaven help her friends..."*

In this photo: Jim Clark
June 14
2 people like this.

Candy ~ *"oops look who's
peekin' in the background ...
lol unintentional."*

Jim ~ "I'm a stalker now... omg... busted :)"

Candy ~ *"there are some things in this world that just
can't be explained... consider this one of them! :)"*

Candy June 15, 2010 at 9:08pm
Re: thinking about...

:)

Candy June 16, 2010 at 12:05 pm
Re: thinking about...

*Hello sunshine of my life :) ... hope there are sane peo-
ple where you are today. Bex has been on the warpath all
night long and still today. I have no clue what set her off,*

but apparently everyone needs to pack up and move. I've been afraid to ask if that included me yet. Throwing and breaking things, I've dodged a few things when she came up the stairs but caught a few too.

Let's put it this way ...if we had a bomb shelter I'd be in it. Don't know what's going on just trying to stay out of her way at this point. Stress is going to kill her I tell you ... it might kill me today if I dont learn to dodge things more quickly lol.

I may have to come back to Florida to stay if this keeps up. Can't handle much of this. She's suppose to be leaving in a little while. Hopefully, I'll catch you when its safe. I'm about as sick as I've ever been today and this isn't helping. Cross your fingers... ttysoon i hope! :)

Candy June 17, 2010 at 8:14am
Subject: Good morning...

Well you didn't snore... snorted a couple times but that's ok.. ;)

Good morning...oh great one who goes above and beyond the call of duty to make sure crazy people survive their messed up lives !

Hope you slept well. I was sleeping very well until ... I smelled food! lol ... Grabbed a couple of bagels and some juice. I'll have them later. (yes I promise)

Right now T.W. is singing to me and the pillow is calling me because it's lonely. So I'll crawl back in for a little while. :)

Thank you for yet one more rescue, and for keeping me company again. I'll never be able to repay you ... but just know this crazy whatever I am loves you. You are my hero.

I will talk to you soon. How about taking care of yourself today??? Hope you have a simply wonderful day. I'll be thinking about you (of course) gonna go snuggle in for a little while.. talk to you in a bit. xoxoxooxoxoxoxoxoxo ♥♥♥♥♥

Love ya ~ Candy

Candy June 17, 2010 at 5:27pm

Re: Good morning...

Everythings taken care of here ... busy all day. Maybe I'll catch you tonight. Going to try to rest a little while. No worries . xo :) ...just tired need to take my meds like a good little girl. Everything is fine . Talk to you soon xo

Candy posted something on my wall writing:

". . . yourself! :) xo"

Candy June 18, 2010 at 3:09am

Subject: :)~

1 am and wide awake ... breaking out the rubber mallot! ... need to sleep. Hope you had a wonderful night. I'm gonna go try this again. I know what it is ...I'm use to looking at our beach until I fall asleep lol. oh well ... taking more meds and snuggling back in. talk to ya soon. xo love you ~~ Candy

Candy June 18, 2010 at 8:40am

Re: :)~

Sounds great ...with the exception of the hot and sweaty part (poor baby) I guess I slept too much after we talked . Wide awake @ midnight and now I'm tired again ...duh! I can't get me together... feeling pretty sick this morning but it will pass. The manager here sent up a bag of bagels and juice. Don't know what that was all about. But then again they all assume my lovely purple and now green eye came from a big burly bad guy beating up little ol' me. (I heard them talking to each other) And in the words of my friend Jim ... whatever! ...lol

I was told to not even attempt to leave until after 8:30 this morning. I'm ready to go ...but Atlanta morning traffic ..no thank you. Now you want to see someone have a panic attack?? lol

Maybe I'll get to talk to you before I leave. Either way I'll keep you updated as I go . I swear, Rae is gonna have heart failure before I get there... worries too much.

I will be fine so no worries... If I need rescueing I'll send up smoke signals or something I promise! :) Taking my meds now so maybe all this pain and nausea will pass. I'll talk to you soon.

I love ya! ~ Candy xo

Well hello what a nice surprise!

On Mon, 6/21/10, Jim Clark wrote:
From: Jim Clark
Subject: u
To: "Candy"
Date: Monday, June 21, 2010, 1:55 PM

Never used this one...

So let's do it today and see what happens...

Happy Monday Candy! Much love and happiness from the crazy guy down the street.

Jim

...

Candy June 22, 2010 at 3:35pm

Subject: :)

Found something from way back when... a better smile than you'll find on me now... the dumb goofy grin.

Thanks for helping me find it now and then. xo

Candy June 23, 2010 at 12:21pm

Re: is it thursday?

of course I screamed your name all night! doesn't mean it was always in pain ... :) I was awake just figured I'd bothered you enough for one day. Just back from the dr. More decisions to make and I have no idea what to do. I'm just so confused...typical day right?

love ya Jim ... what would I do without you? xo

The decision Candy was referring to was if she wanted to start chemo treatments again or not. When we talked about it, she didn't know if she wanted to be burning up from the chemicals affecting her body again.

LUNCH IS SCHEDULED

On June 23rd I found out that Rae was having lunch with Candy next week. I thought this might be the chance I had to meet her in person. I text Rae online and asked her what she thought. She said it could be really good, and that she would let me know where they were going to meet. Rae told me that she was taking her daughter and her daughter's friend shopping at Pier Park. Also, they were meeting Candy there for lunch after her morning doctor appointment.

Candy is looking forward to seeing Rae and states: *"Having lunch with my "super mom" tomorrow... I miss her hugs and smile. Trying to work up the courage to do more ... but I'll do what I can and leave the rest for some-one else to worry about. :)"*

Well, Thursday morning comes and I am excited about meeting Candy for the first time. Sure, I am both scared and anxious not knowing if she will like me in person. I got there early, around ten o'clock, and headed to Borders so I could work online while waiting to hear from Rae. I checked my e-mail, worked on a little ad for a client and sent it out. Not sure what time, but about 11:30 am I saw Rae come to the back of the bookstore. She doesn't see me yet and I didn't want to frighten her by approaching her, so I wait. A little while later Rae saw me and came over to say hello. I gave her a hug and we talked for a couple of minutes. She told me that Candy would be here soon, and that I could continue working until she arrives.

I took a deep breath and sat back down anxiously awaiting her arrival. Rae continued looking around at the books until her daughter and her daughter's friend arrived. They sat at a table close by and talked. Then, I saw Rae on the phone talking, I assumed she was talking to Candy. She smiled at me and I wondered what they were saying. They continued talking for a good while but something seemed strange. Rae got off the phone and came over to tell me what was going on. As she was walking over, I could tell Candy wasn't coming. I just felt it. Rae told me Candy was feeling sick after her doctor's appointment and wasn't going to be able to make it to lunch. She said she was just going to drive home and rest.

Rae asked me if she could take a picture of me with her phone. I said: "yes". She took it and sent it to Candy. I told Rae that it was ok, even though I was really disappointed. Rae returned to where her daughter was sitting and got on the phone again. She called Candy to try to convince her to change her mind. I could see Rae from where I was sitting, she seemed to be getting a little aggravated. Her facial expressions and body language told me she was trying very hard. I know Rae tried her best. Today was not going to be the day for me to meet Candy. I worked some more hoping she would change her mind and come back. She didn't. Rae and the girls came by to say goodbye, I asked them if I could take a picture of all of us with my computer. Rae agreed and the girls said "okay" too. Here is the picture:

When Candy got up from her rest she posted this on facebook: *"I missed a great opportunity today to spend time with people I love. Maybe they will all forgive me. I'm glad they got to meet anyway. Have a good night all xo"*

Candy June 26, 2010 at 12:02pm

Hope you have an amazing weekend. Trying to stay off fbook... but I'll be mobile. Talk to you later. No worries here. Heck I might even eat today! :) have fun. xo ... smooches backatcha xo

 *Don't have a choice i'm stuck in the no refunds no exchanges line in my life. I is what i is...xo*

you always make me smile... here's a real one xo

SECOND CHANCE WITH CHEMO - JUNE 28

Candy ~ *"Decisions, decisions... mint chocolate chip or banana split ice cream... (like I need a brain freeze?!)... for once in my life I can eat all the ice cream I want without worrying about it and of course... I'll dive in knowing the consequences. Gotta gain that weight the dr said today... never thought I'd hear that. Hear goes nothing.... but what a way to go!"*

Candy ~ *"Not looking forward to what I have to face today. But I do so knowing it's a chance I need to take to try to find my way back to living. Chemo is not a pleasant thing to have to begin all over again. But I do so, knowing I'm not alone. Whatever the end result, I will know I have tried once more. I may go out, but I'll go out fighting with a little help from my friends. xo"*

Rae ~ "You are worth fighting for little lady! don't ever forget it! say the word & I'm there."

Candy June 30, 2010 at 8:40 am

Subject: Good morning

Hope the sun is shining in your part of the world.

Started chemo early this morning. I'm so thrilled...can you tell?

Woke up @ 4:30 and you were the first thing on my mind. I wonder why? hmmm... :)

Just wanted to wish you a good day. I will try (and I stress TRY) not to bug you so much today. Have a lovely day. Hope all your dreams come true today.

Love ya much ,

~ Candy xo

Candy June 30, 2010 at 9:04 am

Re: Good morning

Well hello sweet cheeks i needed a smile right about now. left the laptop behind this morning. Thanks for making me smile again and again

...love ya

Candy July 1, 2010 at 9:07 pm

Re: Hey you

You never know stuff happens ...walking again..just not quite so far

Candy July 2, 2010 at 8:48 am

Re: Hey you

No chemo today ...cant get this 103 fever to break so the doc says cant risk sharing it with the other patients. Will try again Monday. More meds yaay me. Going to put the pillow over my head now and see if thats any better . lol ... have a great day. xo my fat ass gained 2lbs ...good grief!

Candy July 4, 2010 at 12:07 am

Re: morning...

"Take me There" still just gets me every time. Thank you Jim. xo

Candy July 4, 2010 at 12:22 am

Re: morning...

Trust me, you don't want to know it all. It's a very ugly place to be. Not a pretty picture of where I've been or the real hell I've gone through. It would explain a lot about why I hide though. It's a hard place to be knowing the real me.

Candy July 4, 2010 at 12:30 am

Re: morning...

I don't wish anything I've been through on anyone.
I love you Jim. xo

Candy July 4, 2010 at 12:36 am

Re: morning...
Thank you for being you xo

Candy July 4, 2010 at 12:04pm

Re: morning...
have a wonderful day today xo
    "Hey Candy from the both of us..."

Candy ~ likes this.

Candy ~ *"Love it ... two of the best on earth ! xo hugs to*
both of you xo"

Candy July 6, 2010 at 10:37 pm

Subject: good night

Busy day tomorrow ... gonna try to sleep. Have a great night. Don't know if I'll be on much tomorrow. I miss you already. :(Take care. Have a lovely day tomorrow. Thinking seriously about calling L..... It was a very sweet thing that she did. I don't know . I guess I will know when I'm ready. Not going to force anything. Thank you for being the man that you are. You make everything so much easier. I'll see you in my dreams tonight. Tired of the nightmares... Gonna FORCE you into my dreams... I'm vicious that way! :) Use the force on me tonight I need it! Have a great night and dont hog the covers...I love you Jim. Good night my sweetest friend. I'm gonna cuddle with you in my dreams, sweet dreams for sure . Talk to you again soon. Love you more xo

Candy July 7, 2010 at 2:01 am

Subject: smoochy smoochy xo

Cant sleep of course ...I did sleep for a couple hours so I won't complain. Had sweet dreams all I can say is mm-mmm.... :) lol Hope you have had a great evening. Maybe I'll get to talk to you tomorrow. Going for some injections to help with the pain in my hip and back after chemo. Fun times. ugh!!... oh well it is what it is.

Maybe I'll make a short phone call tomorrow. I don't know. I can't seem to decide much of anything these days. What do you think?

L's letter was nice. She seems very sweet. I know they are making their efforts. But how do I put all of this on them to begin with? It's not fair to them to get to know me and then I'm gone. I just don't think I can look another person in the eyes that I care about and know that I'll have to look into those same eyes and say goodbye. It hurts too much. My heart breaks thinking what this "thing" is doing to people I care about. I know how it feels to say goodbye to someone before they die and all the hurt and grieving you go through. It kills my heart to know that's what I'm going to do to the people that care about me. I don't like it, but it's my truth. The truth I have to face everyday. I pray for miracle, but I don't have enough faith to see it through. Some things are just meant to be. My heart aches all the time. I'm just so very grateful that you brought me back to my beach. Even if I can't plant my feet in the sand, I can hear it. I can smell it. I can see it. It gives me peace. It calms me down when I get so anxious I can't breathe. Thank you for bringing me back Jim. Thank you for being who you are. You are an incredible man. I love you. xo

Candy July 8, 2010 at 1:53 am

Subject: good night

Sorry oops ... there i go again ..oh well I am anyway that I kind of got a little messed up trying to answer your texts today ...the phone kept ringing and strange people at my door. And I was loopy me. Feeling better though I did get some sleep ...I guess I really didnt have a choice LoL... Anyway thanks for today . Hope you've had a nice evening. Sleep well . Sweet dreams. Talk to you soon. Getting a breathing treatment now for this crazy asthma so I'll be here for a bit. Catch ya later . Love ya xo

Candy July 11, 2010 at 12:37 am

Subject: Hey you...

I forgot to tell you something... yesterday was my weigh in . It's official. I'm a fatty . In the past 2 1/2 weeks I have put on 10 freakin pounds! 115 lbs now. Time to put the breaks on ! Geez ... gonna have to butter my butt to get me through the door in another month at this rate! ... Talk to ya soon xo love ya!

Candy July 16, 2010 at 10:22 am

Subject: Have a lovely day today

Heading home... chemo done. Have a lovely day today and a wonderful weekend. xo Thanks for getting me through another one. Who the heck needs tv ? I have enough drama for everyone! Love ya Jim ...take care ...I'll try not to bug you so much today. xo mwah!

Candy July 16, 2010 at 6:43 pm

Subject: on my way to the er

"I have been all kinds of sick with this chemo thing but I have never had my tummy hurt like this ...it may be food poisoning I don't know... made the mistake of eating some fish and a salad. That didn't last long. I think this is as sick as I have ever been, what ever it is ..it's not good right now. Had to be helped up off the floor. I've got a ride. Gotta go. Send one up for me this is pretty bad right now I am in serious pain . ttul"

This was a scary day. I was working as usual and would get a short message from time to time asking about how my day was going. Then, I got this e-mail titled "on my way to the er" (emergency room). Food poisoning wasn't something I thought Candy would get because of how much she loved to cook. I waited online to hear a message from her saying: "all is good it was just this..." but it didn't happen. Someone else sent me a Yahoo text message from Candy's phone telling me that the chemo was affecting her badly today. The person who sent it said Candy had been throwing up blood and it was not a pretty sight. My heart dropped when I heard of the blood, but I was relieved that Candy wanted someone to let me know what was going on. Still concerned, I sat on pins and needles the rest of the day.

Later that evening, I received a message saying that she needed to rest and she would be ok. Candy contacted me the next morning. This was a rough moment and made me realize that I needed to prepare myself for when "that day" might come. It was hard to think about, so I decided to talk to my friends about it. I knew there was nothing I could do for Candy other than what little bit I was doing, just being here for her when I could. I wish I could have been with her at the emergency room to hold her hand. Or even to make sure that she had made it back home safely. Why was she so stubborn (like me) and not wanting to let me help?

A couple of days later Candy is back to being herself. She's online encouraging others to have a great week and sharing the love.

Candy ~ *"X = a kiss ...O= a hug... It's simple ...every-one needs a kiss and hug now and then. Don't be greedy. Share! lol ... have a great week everyone. May all your dreams be filled with xxx's and OOO's ... Love you xo"*

Raquel ~ "Ya know, that's what everyone says they mean but I always thought it was the other way around for some reason... I always thought "X" meant hugs because you cross your arms and "O" meant kisses because of the o your lips make when you kiss!!! Ha Ha Ha... I know its not standard so I guess I'll keep it dyslexic >giggles< Good Night... Meow LPK"

Candy ~ *"works either way for me... Someone asked me why i always put that xo at the end of my sentence... just sharing the love!"*

Jim ~ "xOxOxOx"

Rae ~ "well don't leave me out!! xoxoxoxoxo"

Candy July 19, 2010 at 3:59 pm
Re: I'm tired of shopping!

you're easy to deal with ... and don't be talking about my jim's face like that either! dont make me put the smack-down on you ... (skeered yet? didnt think so) smoochiesss

Candy July 19, 2010 at 6:38 pm

Re: hummm just thinking 'bout you baby

hmmm ... all I can say about that is ... Good morning to you :)

Candy July 19, 2010 at 6:48 pm

Re: i shouldn't have started looking at music...

I love me some Jim xo

Candy July 24, 2010 at 1:55 pm

Subject: Hoping your weekend is wonderful

I love you Jim. Thank for all the times you have always been here for me. Did I mention I love you? You have seen me through everything. You are truly an incredible man. I carry you in my heart always. xo

Candy July 24, 2010 at 6:44 pm

Re: Hoping your weekend is wonderful

The heart is perfect. Never more perfect than today. I would send you my heart, but you already have it. xo

Candy July 25, 2010 at 11:46 am

Re: Hoping your weekend is wonderful

Grace and Geo are taking me to sit on the beach for a while today. I will cherish every moment of it as I think of you there with me. Thank you for giving it to me again and again when I couldn't be here. You are always with me in my heart. I love you . Just wanted you to know this today.

Candy July 26, 2010 at 4:43 pm

Subject: yes dear

I love you . . . keep smiling. xo

Thank you baby... you always know what I need. xo

July 28th, Candy e-mails me a joke called *"The Porch ..."* (*"from a true blonde who can appreciate it"*)

The Porch (unknown author)

A blonde teenage girl, wanting to earn some extra money for the summer, decided to hire herself out as a 'handywoman' and started canvassing a nearby well-to-do neighborhood. She went to the front door of the first house, and asked the owner if he had any odd jobs for her to do.

'Well, I guess I could use somebody to paint my porch,' he said. 'How much will you charge me?'
Delighted, the girl quickly responded, 'How about $50?'

The man agreed and told her that the paint brushes and everything she would need was in the garage.

The man's wife, hearing the conversation said to her husband,

'Does she realize that our porch goes ALL the way around the house?'

He responded, 'That's a bit cynical, isn't it?'

The wife replied, 'You're right. I guess I'm starting to believe all those dumb blonde jokes '.

Later that day, the blonde came to the door to collect her money.

'You're finished already?' the startled husband asked.

'Yes, the blonde replied, and I even had paint left over, so I gave it two coats.'

Impressed, the man reached into his pocket for the $50.00 and handed it to her along with a ten dollar tip.

'And by the way,' the blonde added, 'it's not a Porch, it's a Lexus.'

Two days before Candy died I received this e-mail. I try to hold back the tears, I can't, because it goes deep into my heart. I didn't feel I had done anything great but knew we were close. I told her that "Always and Forever" was a motto I had adopted and even had it tattooed on my back. It states that I am always going to be true to myself and that she should live this way as well. I wanted her to know that I loved her, was never leaving her, and that she had filled the broken parts in my heart.

Subject: Two of a kind I guess ...

We are both crazy some would say. But I wouldn't trade this kind of crazy for anything. I don't know what will happen in the next few days but I just want you to know that you have made my life so much easier the past few months. I could not have come this far without you. I thank you for all my days at the beach and for filling my loneliest hours with smiles, laughter, music and most of all you! I will carry you with me through eternity. No one will ever be able to comprehend this that is between us. But it has made me very happy to feel that there is one true, genuine person here that could care about a crazy, mixed up, broken, twisted girl like me. I love you Jim Clark and nothing can change that. Thank you for being the man that you are. You not only are in my heart, you ARE my heart. You put the pieces back together so I could feel what some-

*one really loving me for me could feel like. You are with
me always. You have my heart always and forever.*

~~ I love you ~~ Candy xo

On Wednesday, I sent a little e-mail to Candy with
my photo and a very short message to check in with her
followed by her response:

I write: "this guy loves Candy . . ."

August 4th she replies: *"That's
great 'cause Candy love this guy
... xo"*

CHAPTER 15

ANOTHER DAY IN CANDYLAND

"Have a lovely day / weekend everyone... Don't let anyone get you down ! And if you are already down ...grab my hand and I'll pull you on up into Candyland... it's a crazy place to be, but never, ever boring! Love you my FRIENDS!!"

CANDY'S GIFTS

I don't know when Candy decided to send me her journal. Maybe it was when I told her I would never forget her and thanked her for letting me into her life. I'm not sure why, but when she said she was sending me something in the mail it was like Christmas was coming twice this year.

One of the items in the box was a candy dish. It was a crystal snail and it was surrounded by Hersey's chocolate kisses and a box of Andes chocolate mints. We both said we loved almost anything chocolate and the mint chocolate chip ice cream was our favorite. Almost any chocolate, because I didn't like the taste of coffee, and she loved the Mocha Frappe's at Mickey D's. On the way home from Georgia, she said this about one of her favorite drinks: *"I love Mickey D's. Free wifi and they sell happiness in a cup. It's called Mocha Frappe' Happylooyah!!"*

But back to my gift package. I was curious about why Candy chose the snail. When I asked her why she picked it out she told me this: *"I'm as slow as a snail so the choice of the candy dish is definitely me. I hope with every little clink of the dish you smile. It's nothing significant, nothing big. But it's silly just like me."* I told her that our candy dish would never be empty and that every time I opened it I would think of her. There is no way you can not think of her when you do, well, it is impossible for me.

Inside my "Candy Box" were two envelopes addressed to me, but without stamps. Both with *"xo"* on the back of them. I opened the first one and smiled at the sight of two frogs looking at each other. The front of the card read: "Life is so busy. If I could have *five extra minutes* each day..." I opened it to read the inside. It read: "I'd make out with you *like crazy* for five minutes." and Candy signs it: *"And pray for a billion more to match it! - Candy xo"*. We had talked about walking on the beach together, sharing sunsets and a kiss good night.

The other card said a lot more and went straight to the heart of our relationship. It read: "I love the way you know me and things about me *that nobody knows*. The way you can tell when I'm upset or want to talk, *before I even say a word.* The way you know when to let me go or pull me close, *and how you make me laugh* when I feel like I'm losing my mind. I love the way you keep my secrets safe and *my dreams alive.*" and then on the inside: "I love the way it feels to be known and loved, and accepted by you - just as I am." Candy signs it: *"Thank you for just being you! Candy xo"*.

But wait, there's more! The greatest gift in the box smelled like coconuts, yes coconuts. It was a multi-colored journal and Candy had put coconut oil on it for the scent. She said she thought she had ruined it because it had spilled all over the cover. She wanted it scented because it would remind me of the beach, but now I would probably think of sun tan oil. We laughed about it and I told her it was perfect.

The journal, wow, what a gift someone can receive! I opened the journal and ate a piece of candy. I knew I was going to leave the house for a few hours, and once I started reading I wouldn't want to stop. So I took another smell of the coconut oil, put the chocolate kisses in the snail, and took the journal upstairs to my room where I finished getting ready to leave.

After playing cards and hanging out with a few friends I returned home. I have to say, I was both nervous and excited about reading Candy's journal. She had told me it was un-cut, not edited, and that she may have said too much. I told her I didn't care and that it was a gift I would treasure forever.

I placed the journal on my bed and got ready to call it a night. Sure, in the back of my head I knew it was going to be tough to read about a friend and her experiences, but I thought I was ready. I got comfy and picked up the journal. I couldn't help but smile when I smelled the coconut scent again.

Ok, open the book already I said to myself. Well, here goes... I opened to the inside cover and see Candy's name, and on the other side I read this: *"Things I should always remember even if I forget!   :)   Just as crazy as me. Jim thank you for all the smiles, the music and most making this crazy, broken woman feel whole again. I love you"*. Candy's humor makes me smile again followed by a "thank you" I don't feel I deserve.

I turned the page. She talks about how she feels things happen for a reason and that God puts friends here for us. She talks about her friend Rae, and then being diagnosed with bone cancer and a aneurism in her brain. This is followed by words of life before cancer, her relationship with her boyfriend and their future plans, followed by her "hell on earth", being beat up and raped, almost killed, and the murder of her unborn child. I warn you, it is an unforgettable story and hard to read. I wondered how could someone keep on living after being put through all of this. Where does the desire come from? It must come with faith and belief that something better is bound to come out of it all. Then, when you do recover a little, your best friend is killed by a drunk driver. You start to question "why not me?". Candy asks herself: *"They killed my baby. Tore my soul away from me. The Candy that I was died that day. They stole my baby, my personality, my memories, my life. Now every time I try to sleep I relive this hell. Why the hell didn't I die? Why was I left to be tormented day in and day out? Can't sleep because I will go there again. And yet I live."* I did not know what to think. How sad to be in this state mentally without someone close to comfort you. The tears started, but I had to keep reading.

Her life continues with a battle against cancer. The treatments side effects are hard to handle. Candy writes: *"It hurts. I'm afraid to look in the mirror again. The pain. The burning. The nausea. The diarrhea. All the ugliness of cancer and chemo. Now to lose my hair."* Candy called Rae to discuss options. Candy writes: *Rae just left. She brought clippers, scissors and razors. If I was going to lose my hair I will do it on my on terms. This is what I tell myself. I talk to myself more and more these days which sometimes bizarre especially when it's out loud. The hair fell silently to the floor. But my heart felt every strand. Is this what I have let myself become? Hair, makeup and a mani/pedi? My God how superficial am I? Today I am alive. I live. I breathe. For some strange reason beyond my comprehension I am here. Rae says to me as she leave. "Candy today is your blessing. Today you should rejoice that you are up walking, talking and breathing on your own. God has a reason for you to be here. Above all remember your hair did not, does not determine who you are or your self worth."* After Candy's hair is gone she cries, then she laughs saying *"My ears look like friggin' satellite dishes. They are huge..."* Rae and Candy decided it's time to play and got the make-up, earrings, scarves, and hats out to have some fun.

Sleep is one of those things Candy can not focus on. She worries that the men who didn't catch before are still looking for her to finish what they started. She has nightmares, and still has cancer on her mind and in her body. Her emotions are running wild. Here is a sample of her thoughts: *"I'm so freaking emotional today I don't know what to do with myself. I'm pissed at the world. The world didn't do this to me. But sure feels like it. I don't want to see, smell or hear anyone today. I'm so fucking tired of all of this bullshit called life."* It said *"smell"* because she said she would never forget the smell of the breath of the men abusing her. I wonder what could make a person be so evil to another human. She writes: *"I can't remember their faces but I remember their stinking breath. I remember their hands. Their laughter cheering each other on to do it again. I remember their stinking drunken bodies it makes me vomit again. I rolled out of bed screaming, crying, shaking. I need some one to talk to, someone to distract me. I'm afraid to move. It's feeling like they are always watching me."* This made me sick and I wanted to stop reading but I can't. I need to know as much as I can to talk to her tomorrow and continue helping my friend live.

Candy's anger is visible. She is mad at everything but still wants to, needs to, get it out, at least on paper. I'm sure it helps a little. She writes: *"The chemo burns me up. Feels like my skin is on fire. My belly is burning like someone poured gasoline down my throat and set it on fire. This is just messed up. I throw up again but there's nothing there. It hurts like hell. I wish I would just die. I hate what this has done to me. I hate what I've become. A million people it seems have a million different ways I should deal with this. None of these ass holes are dealing or have dealt with this. I don't give a shit how many times you've read about it until you live it yourself you don't have a fucking clue. Why don't they just shut the fuck up? Well meaning as they think they are some days I just need them to shut the hell up and give me a hug."*

I wish it was as easy as that. Rae knew how to say what Candy needed to hear and how to comfort her. Candy says: *"Except for Rae she's the only one who walks in armed with her "goodies" for me as she calls them, says not one word but comes to me, puts her arms around me kisses my forehead and just holds me. Not one word for a long time. Lets me cry or say nothing for the longest time then I hear her say softly "I love you Candy". Followed by what can I do for you today? I don't know what it would take to get this treatment from anyone else. Rae's just the best."*

Candy's doctor had recommended that she talk to people on Facebook and not to just shut down. She says: *"That's where I met Rae so it's not all bad. I met Jimmy there one night when I was at my lowest. I wasn't planning on seeing another day. All my pill bottles. The meds-lovely meds. Pain, muscle relaxer, xanax, my fruit loop medicine all lined up in a row. Lids off. Lovely bottle of Crown Royal and a bottle of chilled wine. And the loaded .38 all by the bed. This was gonna be the night I showed up on Facebook in a stupor reading mindless posts from strangers. I decided to go play a little in YoVille. What the hell? Jimmy talked to me. Talked me down he had no clue. So here I am to die another day. Jimmy became my habit, made me think he loved me. I'm so damn vulnerable so gullible. I'd listen to anything. I miss the thought of being loved but I'm afraid to see anyone face to face. I'm just fucked! My new word for my life."*

Candy talks about Jimmy, how she had met him on Facebook and how they talked about getting together for Christmas. But she states: *"He also says his words "If you make it until December we will talk about our life together." What the fuck? Really? If? But I am to go to New Mexico for Christmas. Why?"* After this I don't think they talked much, if at all, I am not sure.

Then, I see my name in the journal. I guess God wanted me there to help out in whatever way I could. The journal reads: *"Time to write again? Maybe? Jim says yes!"* She wrote that I said it was time to start writing again. Candy had told me she felt like there was so much in her head she wanted to get out. I told her to get a journal and start writing whatever came to mind. She told me she had already started one, but had stopped for some reason. We talked about the writing I had been doing, and how I enjoyed writing when I made time for it. She said that time was something she had, but didn't know how much of it she had left.

Then she talked about the times we spent talking together while she was taking chemo treatments. We talked about life, music, and about the times I brought the beach to her. She loved the beach. I decided that I would send a

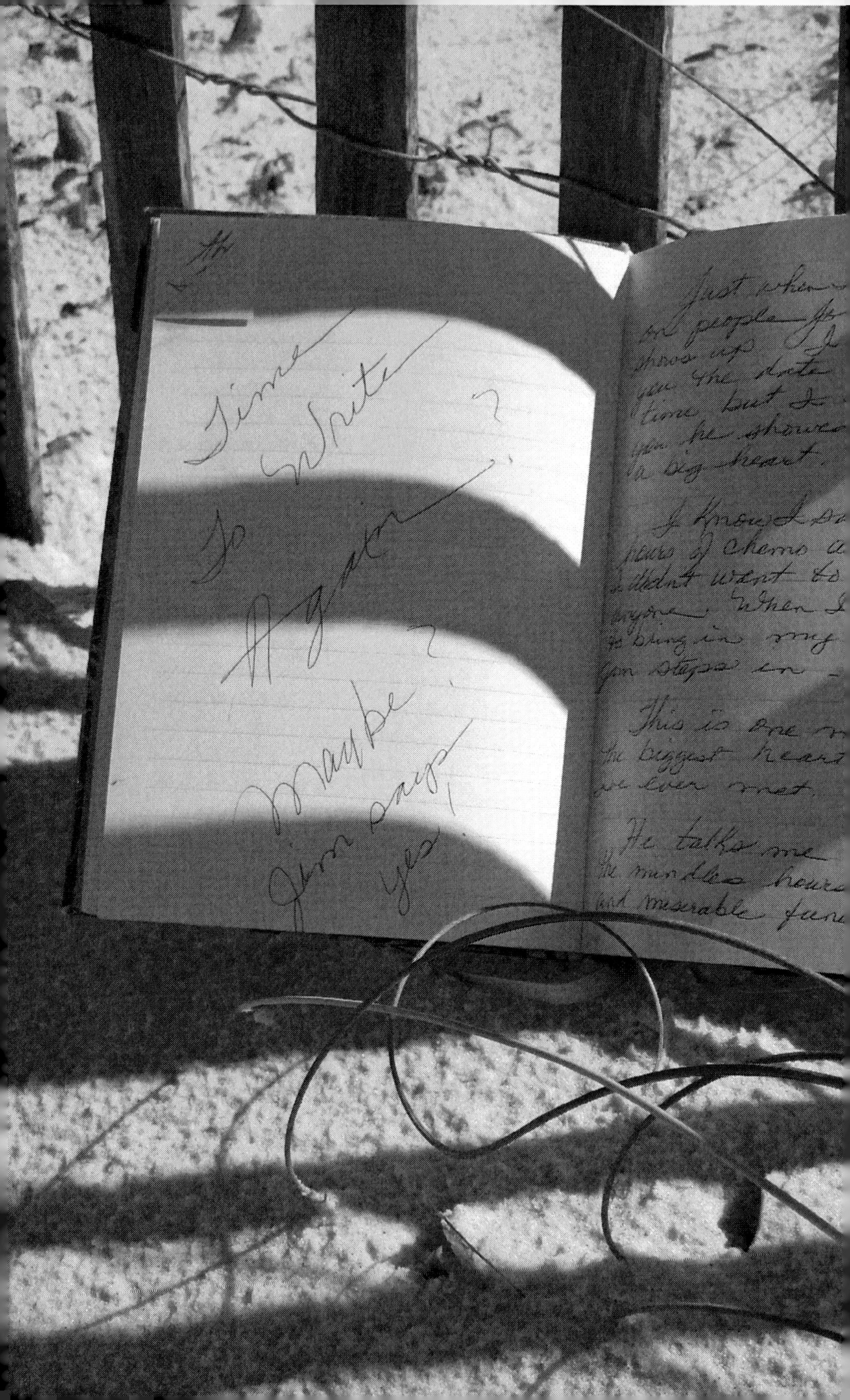

Time
To
Write
Again?
maybe?
Jim says
yes!

little bit of the beach to her instead of just pictures. I wanted to send something she could see, feel, touch, taste, and smell. So, I put together my "I Care" package. It included a painting of a beach scene, a bottle of "Relax" wine filled with beach sand, some starfish, shells, and some music. I can't remember if I noted on the painting "Our Beach" or "Candy's Beach", I need to ask Rae because Candy gave it to her right before she passed. I wrote a line or two on the back as well.

With Candy in Georgia, I felt that there was never going to be a chance for me to meet her in person. My brother and his family moved close to Atlanta because of his job. This gave me a little hope knowing I would have a place to stay if I did get a chance to meet her in person.

I didn't know the real story behind what was really happening in Georgia. Bex was stressed with work and now taking care of her sick friend. In Candy's journal this was written: *"I hate Georgia. I'm miserable. Bex is drinking more and more. Becoming more agitated with me. She came into my room drunk and asked me "Why don't you go ahead and fucking die already?" This isn't the Bex I know. I'm killing her with this thing that consumes me. It's now consuming her. It does everyone that cares about me. Eventually they all leave. My God I don't want to hurt anyone this way."* I wish I had known what was happening, I would have been more persistent to help.

Candy survived another stressful evening and wrote more about me. I feel a little strange talking about myself but I'll get over that. That's what writing memoirs are all about, right? Candy says that *"I keep her happy"*, *"Jim keeps me sane. Keeps me happy. Makes sure I've eaten."* These things made me smile when I read them.

Then, when I am at another advertising federation conference, Candy decided to get another tattoo. She posts a photo of it online and waited for my reaction. You already read about it in the AD3 chapter, it was a good day.

Candy makes the decision to come back to the beach. Things were getting a little rough for her and one evening she told me that she is going to a hotel. I didn't know what was happening, but knew that I wanted her safe, and if she didn't feel safe there she needed to leave. We had been talking on the computer when she told me that *"tonight was the night to go"*, that she would head to the Hampton Inn, which was just down the street. I told her to text me when she arrived. She said it shouldn't take long because she already had her stuff packed. Her journal said: *"Packing my bags only 2 don't have much. My painting, a few books and my beach, meds and shake mix"* followed by *"Safe at the Hampton Inn., Jacuzzi woohoo!, Where's Jim*

when I need him tonight? Online waiting to see if I'm ok of course." After I received a *"Jacuzzi"* text, I knew she was good for the evening. We talked for about an hour more, I asked what her plans were, if she needed me to come get her, and to be in touch along the way if she was driving herself. Candy assured me that she could stay with Mom and Pops at the condo.

The next entry made me smile because I could imagine her smiling as she is driving towards the beach. Heading *"home"* to Florida she writes: *"For so long I stressed over not knowing where home was. Now I know. Home is where you leave your heart at the end of the day. Home is where you want to be when the whole world just sucks. Such profound words Ha Ha. The closer I am to Jim and Rae the closer I am to home. Haven't been gone long and already another stop... Not gonna stress I'm on my way. If it takes me a week I don't care I'm going home! I will feel even closer to Rae and Jim. I'm just gonna crawl up in their hearts and stay. It's safe and comfortable there. It's the only place I feel like I belong. They always make room for me there. I'm going home."* Candy stopped at Mickey D's along the way to use the bathroom, pick-up a Caramel Frappe, and to touch base with me and other online friends. This was a good thing because I would get updates of her trip while working. She even stopped to change a grandma's car tire because, how she put it:

"Dickhead men wouldn't offer to help. That's ok it's done and she's on her way." So Candy! Candy says that the Hathaway Bridge lights looked like a *"Welcome Home Candy"* sign.

Candy's back in Florida and I want to try again to meet her in person. The drive to say hello and give her a big hug is better knowing that she is just down the street less that 30 miles. I talked about it with her but I didn't want to pressure her 'cause she has been through enough lately.

I read more and wish things had been different. I know the outcome would have been the same, but I could have spent more time being there for her. She could have smiled and even laughed more. I could have taken her to the beach, "our beach", a few more times. Knowing now what she had written in this journal, my gift, I would have done some things differently. Candy wrote this after taking a long walk: *"Need a shower then a nap. Damn I hurt. My hip is killing me. Where's Jim? Rub my hip. Damn I know he would. Why am I such a spazz? The only man in the world I know won't hurt me and I won't let him see me. Not his fault, God knows he tries. I don't mean to seem cruel. I just can't stand the thought of looking into one more persons eyes that I'll have to say goodbye to. Especially his eyes. God I love his eyes. I love Jim. What I wouldn't give to snuggled up in his arms tonight. I'm such an idiot. I would love to just take one walk on the beach, our beach, with him, watch the sunset and just hold onto him until I fall asleep. One thing for sure. There would be no nightmares. He would find a way to keep them away. I would drift off to sleep just breathing him in. Listening to his heart beat. Listening to his breathing. Just feeling safe in his arms. Damn I love this man."* Well, we did talk about doing these things together, holding hands while watching the sun set, listening to live music, having a glass of wine, and then her falling asleep on my chest. If it helped her keep the nightmares away for just one night, then it was worth it.

Next in the journal comes "The Family". You read about in chapter 12, it's a bumpy ride to say the least. Father's Day, the way her father reacted when she contacted him, a family she didn't know had existed and her feelings towards them. How could someone treat their own child like that and sleep at night? This section makes me mad every time I read it. I can not get what's said out of my head. But I guess it stays there to remind me of the "right" way to treat people. I have to find something good out of it, but it's very hard to.

Back to the good stuff. Please. I read more about what I think is Candy's struggle of whether or not to meet me in person. She writes: *"Jim what would I do without you?*

You get me through another day and give me hope. Make me smile. Make me know I'm not alone anymore. You love me. You always tell me you love me. You make me laugh. You make me smile. You give me strength when I have none. You put back pieces of this ragged old crushed heart. You ease my mind. You give me peace. You tell me you are here holding my hand during chemo. I know you are. I feel you here. I feel your heart."

I told her that I was there with her holding her hand so she wouldn't feel like she was alone. I felt like I was there because we would text most of the day. I think she enjoyed my company and I remember her calling me her *"new addiction"* and her *"Candy Crack"*. This made me laugh and helped me realize I was doing good. Don't get me wrong, she was helping me out quite a bit too. Business was slow and people didn't even want to talk about new projects at this time. So Candy was a good escape and companion for me as well.

I kept reading more about me and how Candy felt about me. It's very hard to read without the tears coming. She tells me that nothing else matters but love, followed by pages of her pouring out her heart in words. She tells me about how I was her rock, her shoulder to lean on, her confidant, and that I was there when the rest walked away. I wished we had more time together, I could have said or done more.

Candy goes on talking to me, letting me know that she will be okay. She wrote things for me to continue doing to be happy and to know that I am loved. Then, she tells me the places I will continue to find her while I am here on earth. She thanks me for letting her into my heart. She had told me this before, and I let her know that she had filled a couple of the holes in my broken heart too.

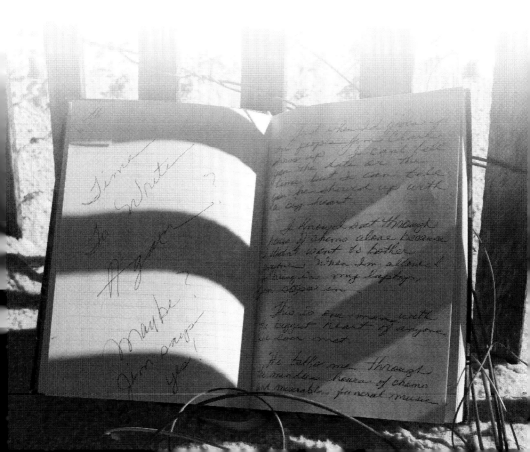

CHAPTER 16

SHARING CANDY WITH STRANGERS

"There are some people who can make you smile ...even when you are at your lowest. Thanks Jim & ladies :) xo"

One day, I was having lunch and checking my e-mails and Facebook messages at Johnny Rockets. After receiving my cheeseburger, I see a little smile made in catsup by the server (pictured above). I thought Candy would enjoy seeing it too, maybe it would put a smile on her face. So I took a picture of it with my phone and posted it online. While doing this, my server Christine asks me what was I was doing and if everything was alright. I told her about Candy and the battle she is going through.

I decided to ask her if she, and maybe the other servers, would like to say hi to Candy as well. She said: "let me check" they said yes, so I got my computer ready and took our group photo. I sent it to Candy who says it was *"so sweet"*. I told her it was nothing but me acting like a fool. Candy told me to continue being *"you"* because it's a good thing for her. The servers asked me to let them know if there was anything they could do to help, and that they would keep Candy in their thoughts.

I enjoy playing cards at Quig's, a local sports bar in Destin. This picture is of some of the folks who play there. I told them about Candy, discussed her progress, and still today we talk about how people should help others.

Even after she passed, still today people continue to ask me how she is doing. I just tell them that she is in a much better place now, and that she would like them to go enjoy a chocolate martini for her. They smile, and right there, I realize Candy's helping another person.

CHAPTER 17

AFTER THOUGHTS

People have asked me if I would do it again, if it was worth spending time with someone knowing that it would only be a short time before they were gone, and what made me do it.

Well, as far as if I would do it again, the answer is "yes". It was a journey into another person's life. I was there to hear her story, to share time together, to talk about past experiences, and discuss "what if things were different" dreams. On top of that, Candy was a new friend, and we tend to spend more time with new friends trying to get to know them and letting them get to know us as well. And, "yes" I have very deep feelings for this lady. I still think about her when I am talking to other ladies. I wonder what she would have said, or how she would have acted under the same circumstances. How she would have been with me while hanging out with friends.

When I first meet Candy, I didn't know how long her battle against cancer was going to be. It could have been many months or years. All I knew was that she was starting another treatment, and she needed people around her to give her support. And, who doesn't need support these days? Having the opportunity to help her may have been a way to help myself. But once I got to know her and her spunky personality, I knew I was staying for the whole "bumpy" ride. (Like she used to refer to her life)

I was able to provide some things that others had tried, but didn't wanted to continue doing when they felt there was no future. I was able to talk to her when she was screaming in pain, but still typing that she would be ok. We were able to joke about it trying to get her mind off it even for a second. I told her to scream my name and she would laugh, because she knew the people outside the condo could hear her. I asked her to think one of her big fluffy pillows was me, and to squeeze it anytime she needed a hug.

Candy said: *"You don't have to be so extravagant in your giving... the quiet, little things no one else sees you do ...can change one person's whole world for the good. Don't be afraid of the silly, little, insignificant things. It might just what they need to turn tears into laughter. (I should know :) I'm an expert in that department) xo"*

On July 30th, Candy changed her status to say the following: *"Blessed sometimes is the one with the unquench-able thirst, because they are always seeking just a little more, just a little better. Never being satisfied with just a sip... Enjoy your life and don't be satisfied with that tiny little sip... Drink it all in and have no regrets... Hope your cup overflows with blessings today and always. xo"* She was always wanting others to be happy and would encourage them to do so.

Candy would tell me and the world about her Ninja Turtle Boxers *"on the balcony wearing my glow in the dark ninja turtle boxers... (don't want to get lost in the dark)... sipping on something ...cold (and yet warm)... music cranked up ... attempting to eat... candles burning..."* *now all I need is...* and how comfy they were. I would joke with her and told her they sounded "soooooooo hooootttttt" and I wished I had a pair of them.

A little before she had left this world she had asked Rae to give me another gift package. Rae brought two gift bags to a "Young a Heart" luncheon at my parent's church. The "Young at Heart" is a group for persons 55 years old and older; mom had asked me to emcee the talent show, and in exchange, she would feed me lunch... ha ha ha, not a bad deal. I told Rae we should meet there, since it's close to where she lived.

I saw Rae come into the fellowship hall, I went up to her to give her a hug, we both needed one. It was the first time we saw each other since Candy was gone. We went

Message Window: candykist1980

you didn't tell me what love means?

candykist1980

haven't figured it out yet

juststaycom

i don't think anybody really does... it is different for every person

candykist1980

its that smile on my face when theres no one around ...you put it there

juststaycom

yes that's little bit of it...

candykist1980

its laughing out loud remembering something you said when im all alone
its you getting me through hours of chemo and giving me the beach while im there

juststaycom

awww baby
i love making you smile

candykist1980

its you holding my hand when im falling apart and being to tell me its ok until i can fall asleep
look in the mirror
you'll see it

juststaycom

to our table, talked for a little, and then I looked inside the gift bag filled with tissue paper. The first thing I touched was a envelope with a "The Art of Friendship" card inside. I opened it and it reads: *"Jim you've perfected the art of friendship and made me love you. I am never alone because of you. Here with me tucked away in my heart. Loving you for an eternity, Candy xo"* There I was, sitting with strangers at church and I started getting teary eyed. I looked over to Rae and smiled.

I can do this, I thought to myself. After blinking to hold back the tears, I looked into the bag and saw a book and realized it was another journal. It was a black and white book like the little kids would have used in preschool. I opened it and saw that it was filled with more of Candy's writing. When I saw this, I told Rae that it would have to wait because I was not crying at this church event.

I looked into the second gift bag and saw another envelope. I took another card out and this one read: *"Smiling yet? You didn't need a "Cowabunga" experience. This is more suited for you! Love You Forever, Candy xo"* (referring to her Ninja Turtle Boxers). Under the card was a pair of "Family Guy" boxers with Stewie on them and printed on them read: "I'm A Bad Boy". I laughed and showed everyone at the table. Rae said: "Well that's Candy for you" and I said: "yup, it is". There was a red coffee cup with

"Hunk of Burning Love" on one side and "It's Good to be King" on the other. And of course, more candy, Werther's Original and Dove Peanut Butter Chocolates. Last but not least, inside the bag, wrapped up in plain off-white paper, was a starfish spangled ornament. Written on the paper was: *"Sorry Sweetie, I'm keeping the one on my pillow. Just figured I could "hang" out with you sometime. Love you, Candy xo"*. Candy had a beach motif bedding set and the pillow case she would hug had a starfish printed on it. People at the table asked me if it was my birthday and I told them it sure felt like it. Then, me and Rae took a little time to share Candy's story with the others at my table.

REMEMBER ME

Candy wanted everyone to remember her this way: *"When I die, I hope people will remember me with a smile, glass of wine and a sarcastic comment twinkling in my eyes...~~ just hope you remember me and smile! xo :)* ♥♥♥ "

On August 5th I had to go to Mobile, Alabama. I was there doing a favor for my friend Jake, who was vacationing in New York. I drove his car to the dealer to be serviced and was waiting for it to be done. I got a message from Rae asking me if I had heard from Candy this morning, which I responded: "nope, not today". Sitting in the waiting room, I wondered if everything was alright with her and what was she up to this morning. Rae messaged me back, letting me know she would get with me if she heard from Candy before I did. The work on the car is completed, and I head out for lunch before going home. While driving across the Mobile Bay Bridge, I looked up to the sky, saw a cloud shaped like a heart and smiled, then it hits me. Candy must have died today, this was a sign from her to let me know that it was ok, she was ready to go.

When I arrived back in Destin, I went to one of my "offices" before going to play cards. When at Panera, I got a message from Rae letting me know that Candy had indeed died. I now knew she was in a better place, a place with no more suffering, no more pain. Then, I realized that yesterday was the last day I got to talk to her. I wanted more. I felt my eyes start to water up and I had to keep myself together. I can do this. It was sad finding out she was gone, losing her too soon, I didn't want this friendship that just started to end. Rae let me know that Candy had passed away at the condo around 1 pm, and that she was now no longer in pain. I posted this on Candy's page to inform all of her friends: "Candy passed away today around 1pm after her long battle with cancer... She will miss all of her friends but wants you to know she will see you again at the beach. RIP Candy ! ! !" along with this video: "Mariah Carey; Boyz II Men - One Sweet Day". A very hard thing

for me to do knowing that she is gone, still waiting for a
" :)" to show up in the comment section on Facebook.

Ernie posts: "to rachel and all of candy's friend's and
family in fla., there's a group of us in ga. that have been in
prayer for candy, and now that this blessed child has gone
home, we pray for you. peace. ernie". Rae says: "Never
gone from our hearts. Save us a seat next to you. Above
all Candy ... dance baby dance!!! We'll see you on the
beach and always in our dreams. I am blessed to have had
such an angel in my life. I love you forever my dearest
sweet friend... xo". And Larry posts: "So sad, there are no
words,,,,,,,,,,,,".

During that day I expected to get an e-mail or message
from her, but knew it was not going to happen. I posted a
video on her Facebook page to make myself feel better.
It doesn't really help, but I told her I would be okay and
I will for her. Earlier that week, I had asked Candy if she
wanted me to continue her Facebook page for her when
she was gone. She said *"yes"*, so from time to time, I post
comments in there for her.

I asked some of Candy's friends on Facebook if they
wanted to tell me anything about her, and Sasha told me
this: "The only thing that I can think of to contribute is
whenever things went wrong or were bad Candy always

sent me a cat hug or a picture of a cat etc...and since she has died, every time something bad has happened 2, not 1 but 2 lost kittens have showed up at my house so I know she is still here with me..xoxo"

Candy continues sharing her love by asking Rae to post a song for me. On August 21st Rae states: "Included in a letter was this date, not to be done before 11 pm, but requested that I post this song for you... I don't think I have to say any more. I don't know why this date in particular but I hope it helps. You know she loves you for an eternity. :) xo"

MUSIC VIDEO OF ALICIA KEYS - "NO ONE"

I guess it was because we had spent a lot of good times together around 11 pm each night. The lyrics to this song are beautiful and full of emotion. And without being too corny, "No One" can take that away from me. Oh well, it was corny and who cares.

TAKING PHOTOS FOR THE BOOK

I enjoy photography as an escape, for fun, for work. The photos in this book will always remind me of my friend. I hope you enjoy these pictures as much as I did taking them. The photo on the cover and the others in the beginning pages where taken on "Our Beach" as we used to say. The bagel picture was taken at one of the many places I would go talk to Candy online while working. I also included another one with a bird on a dock on a calm bay in Panama City. I used this picture to represent the lake that Candy had enjoyed in her life, and her friends who lived around it.

I took pictures of Candy's journal at the beach because it was the place she loved to go to. Candy wrote: *"Without a Wonderful ending the beginning means nothing ... Thank you for all things Wonderful xo"*. She also surprised me by adding her personal touch with a lipstick kiss.

CONCLUSION

How does it end? I don't think it ever does. Sure, we all live our lives and then some day we are gone from this earth. I feel that if you live a good life, and are good to those around you, positive things will happen. I think a little bit of each of us rubs off on each other. We touch the lives of others, and for better or worse, we will remain there forever in their minds. They will continue to talk about us and our experiences to their family and friends. They will take what they have learned and share it with others. And, if you have really touched the heart and soul of someone like Candy did mine, you will want to share it with others whenever you can.

Sometimes we never miss a good thing until it's gone. Candy told me not to miss her, but it's impossible not to. Every time I go to the beach, "Our Beach", take a trip and take pictures, hear Wayman Tysdale's music playing (another person who left us too soon too), or friends ask how she is doing, I miss her. I still love the "broken girl" from down the street. I am honored to have had the chance to make someone's life better even if we never met in person. Someday, I will get to sit next to her and talk about the crazy stuff we shared, this time face to face. I'll be saying: "Candy remember when we..."

Pictured here is the last message (Y! Messeger) I received on my phone from Candy, it was on August 5th at 7:48 am and read: *"I love you my jim... Thank you for always being there for me. See you on the beach... Xoxoxo"* And the response I hope she got.

AUTHOR'S NOTE

Even though this is a work of fiction to some people, many of the events are very real. I did have conversations with a truly living woman even though I am not sure all the things we talked or wrote about were factual. All I know is that a very good friend of mine did pass away from cancer, and that she is missed by many more people than just myself. I do take what is said to me with a grain of salt, but if the joke was on me with this relationship, then it was a very good one, and I hope someone plays it on me again in the future. I am not 100% sure Candy was her real name, but she was the sweetest thing that happened to me in 2010.

As far as my writing style, you are not going to hurt my or my editor's feelings if it's not up to your standards. I tend to write in a conversational way, if that's a style at all. It's just me talking to you. If you like what I say, or are even interested in reading more that's great. With this being my first book, I am just excited to see it come to print, to be able to share my experience of "Making Friends with Candy" with others and fulfill a promise to a girl I never met in person.

If you did enjoy it, or have any questions, you can e-mail me at: jim@makingfriendswithcandy.com. I will get back to you as soon as I can. If you didn't like it, you most likely didn't make it this far in the book. I still hope you have a great day, week, month, year, life... :)

CHAPTER 18

THE JOURNAL - CANDY'S GIFT TO ME

I hope you enjoy reading Candy's journal, getting to know her, knowing that she is in a much better place today. She was loved, and she will live on through many of us. This is "The Un-edited Version" Candy said, followed by: "I hope you don't think I am crazy."

page 1   signed
Candy Angel Noelle Christmas

page 2   blank

page 3
Things I should always remember even if I forget!

:)

Just as crazy as me.

**Jim thank you for all the smiles, the music and most making this crazy, broken woman feel whole again.
I love you**

page 4   blank

page 5
I will always believe people come into our lives for a reason. I'm not a big believer in fate. For whatever reason, God seems to either place people in your lives

to help you along the way or allows them to come into your life to show you just how strong you can be when you come out on "the other side".

I am grateful for the friends God has placed here for me. I have to believe it was some form of divine intervention, because there seems to be no other explanation for it.

After going through hell on earth and coming out on the other side only to be

page 6

faced with more adversity... This demon called cancer, I've made two of the most wonderful friends on earth.

First there's Rachel who for some strange reason befriended me from hello.

She was in touch with me before I found out about the cancer. I was having horrible headaches that would never go away. At her first urging I finally said something to my doctor who completed a battery of tests and found an aneurism on my brain. Yes! I have a brain... Some days that's questionable.

The doctor sent me to

page 7

Gainesville where after more tests they found a brain

tumor the size of a golf ball. They could take care of the aneurism but the tumor was in a place where there's a 90% chance I would be paralyzed and be left a vegetable - No Thank you!

After bloodwork and more tests - always tests! It showed I have Ewings parcoma - bone cancer.

Who's on the phone before and after? Rachel. I call her Rae. She needs to stand out a bit!

After I told her the news her first words were, "You don't have to do this alone". She's been

page 8

with me every step of the way. Coming back home she was there to meet me. Just like a mom, soups, juices, Hugs & Kisses. Anything I needed.

Rae would leave her family and come running to me when she just got "that feeling" that something was wrong.

Many times after the chemo started I would be lying in a bloody mess on the floor where I'd fallen.

Never one lecture. Never a cross word. Always we (meaning she) will take care of this. Cleaning me up putting me back into bed.

page 9

That's just the kind of person she is. On "chemo days" I would come home to everything set up within reach where I would do nothing other than slip into bed. Juice, soup, shakes, a cooler full of damp wash cloths with ice packs to keep them cool. The chemo always seems to set me on fire.

Rae calls it my "little hot mama" syndrome. She can always find a way to make me laugh, to smile. Some days she tells me to look through her eyes and I will see

page 10

the hope for tomorrow.

Some days it's hard to find that hope but I try.

Some days I just want it to be over. I want the pain to stop. I just want the nausea to stop. I just want to go to sleep and never wake up again.

Sleep. That's another story. Ever since October I've been afraid to sleep. When I sleep the nightmares come then I relive those 4 days of hell all over again. October. I used to love the month. It meant cooler weather. Fall. Leaves turning colors, God showing off his fabulous artwork on

page 11

the hillside. Halloween, parties, children laughing, having so much fun but now when I see even the mention of October to me it's when I died the first time.

My God why didn't you let them finish me off. Some days my anger overtakes everything I know to be right and true.

John and I were planning on being married. We were together for 3 years and were finally going to make it legal. Things when they were good were

page 12

really good. He was there for me when mom died. Held my hand through it all.

I was modeling and he worked as an engineer in construction. We lived very comfortably had a home together. Then things began to change.

Jazmyn helped me to see that drugs had taken over and since I had found out I was pregnant 4 months before John had changed.

It was drugs. I found them it seemed, hiding everywhere.

I had packed my bags early in the morning because Wednesday

page 13

John wasn't due home until Friday. I knew it was getting more dangerous for me and the baby to stay and I had to leave.

I came home to get my things and just leave peacefully or so I thought.

To my surprise John and his 5 friends were there.

Cars parked behind the house, so I didn't see them.

Meth was being cooked in my kitchen.

They were all just crazy!

page 14

John was angrier that I'd ever seen. He had found mine and the baby's things packed and was burning them in the fireplace and the backyard. The only photos that remained of mom and my portfolio, my journals, baby clothes, the crib broken and burned as I was forced to watch.

John grabbed me by my hair slammed me against the wall and told me that he would decide who would have me and my bastard child.

page 15

He passed me around to his friends who took turns raping me and beating me. Laughing and spitting in my face.

I remember John picking up his favorite Louisville Slugger baseball bat and hitting me across the head and back with it. The rest is kind of a blur I've either blocked it out or forgotten it completely. I lost a lot of memory due to the head trama. This went on until Saturday. Then came Jazmyn.

page 16

I vaguely remember Jazmyn kicking the door open picking up a chair and she hit John over the head and dragged me out taking me to the hospital. I'm so angry as I write this now. But I need to remember where I've come from.

I can't remember the names or the faces of the 5 friends, so I could not identify them.

John and one of his friends were arrested

page 17

in South Carolina - Meth Lab - Surprise!

He was charged also with Kidnapping, Domestic Violence, Attempted Murder, Involuntary Manslaughter these he confesses to. No trial just straight to prison.

Prison where one of his buddies sharpened a toothbrush stabbed him in the jugular with it and killed him instantly. His death was quick mine is slow and painful. It's not fair!

page 18

They killed my baby. Tore my soul away from me. The Candy that I was died that day. They stole my baby, my personality, my memories, my life.

Now every time I try to sleep I relive this hell.

Why the hell didn't I die? Why was I left to be

page 19

tormented day in and day out?

Can't sleep because I will go there again.

And yet I live.

After recovering in the hospital Jazymn brings me to Mom & Pops place on Panama City Beach in November. John & the boys won't find me here she says but all I can think is they know me and I don't know them.

page 20

I'm always watching over my shoulder wondering when they'll find me and finish me off.

Now I wish they would. Afraid to live. Afraid to die. What kind of life is this? It's fucked up that's what it is. What has this turned me into? I never talked like that before. Now I'm

page 21

too friggin' tired to care. Jazz got me here. Still takes care of me to this day.

Jazmyn was hit and killed by a drunk driver in November. My one and only true friend. Most of my memories gone with her. Wish I could remember. Life is so fucking frustrating. There's that damn word again.

page 22

What the hell have I become? Have I become so jaded that I have lost respect for myself as well as this so called life?

Some days I can remember nothing of my past. But when I so exhausted for days without sleep. I am forced to sleep. The nightmares come. And I relive it again.

page 23

Why did you leave me here?

What reason is there to take my baby and not take me too?

Why did you take Jazmyn?

Why did you leave me behind?

Was I so bad that you chose to torture me?

I don't understand.

Please give me a sign. Anything, Something!

page 24

I don't recognize my own face today. It seems foreign to me. Someone I don't know.

I woke up. Lifted my head off the pillow leaving half of my long blonde locks behind.

It's only hair I tell myself.

It's proof that the chemo is hard at work.

Blah Blah Blah Blah Blah!

Idle words falling on my own deaf ears.

It hurts. I'm afraid to look in the mirror

page 25

again. The pain. The burning. The nausea. The diarrhea. All the ugliness of cancer and chemo. Now to lose my hair.

It makes me sick to my stomach. I call Rae after thinking about it for a while.

I run my fingers through brittle, chemo burned hair. It falls to the floor.

I call Jimmy who seems to be understanding, his mother had already gone through this.

I wonder about him. About this so called us. That's another story.

page 26

Rae just left. She brought clippers, scissors and razors.

If I was going to lose my hair I will do it on my on terms.

This is what I tell myself. I talk to myself more and more these days which is sometimes bizarre especially when it's out loud.

The hair fell silently to the floor. But my heart felt every strand.

Is this what I have let myself become? Hair, makeup and a mani/pedi?

page 27

My God how superficial am I?

Today I am alive. I live. I breathe. For some strange reason beyond my comprehension I am here.

Rae says to me as she leave. "Candy today is your blessing. Today you should rejoice that you are up walking, talking and breathing on your own. God has a reason for you to be here. Above all remember your hair did not, does not determine who you are or your self worth."

page 28

So for now, I will stop whining, take one more look in the mirror and breathe. Keep breathing. Sometimes I forget to breathe.

Time to look in the mirror.

BREATHE CANDY BREATHE!

At first I cry. Candy is gone forever. But I have to laugh. My ears look like friggin' satellite dishes. They are huge. And my crazy bumpy head would make Connie Conehead jealous/ Damn it's huge!

page 29

I call Rae. She tells me, no more tears for today. Save them for something more drastic.

I asked her if she even looked at this funky head?

She laughs. I laugh hysterically. Rae say it's time to play.

Pull out the makeup and the funky earrings I've been afraid to wear. Grab a scarf, try on some hats and just have fun.

Only Rae could make me find fun in this. Play up your eyes she says I'm thinking Rae's on the juice but it's funny so I'm playing.

page 30

I look like Ronald McDonald with no hair.

Nothing looks right. Gotta shake this off. Can't go though the rest of this fight obsessing over things that will not change.

Mom & Pops have been great to me, moved me out here by the lake

page 31

with them where it's peaceful and quiet. Out of the condo on the beach where it's been over run by spring breakers and left my nerves on edge.

It's quiet. Sometimes too quiet. After all the lake folks have gone to work, Mom & Pops gone to take care of the condos and motel. It's just me, this crazy cat and a yapping yorkie.

The cat gives me an evil glare jumping up on me as I lay in bed staring at me as if she knows way too much. It's those crazy eyes that greet me at 2 am, 3 am or whenever she feels like. I've never figured out how she gets in after I've put her out about what seems fifty times. I think it's Jazmyn playing tricks on me. This strange cat shows up when I'm at my lowest point. Should name the silly thing Jazz it's just as crazy.

page 32
Focus Candy Focus!

Slept for all of 30 minutes, woke up to nightmares again. How can I fight this demon Cancer, when I can't kill these demons from my past this damn October that killed the best part of me. Or was it the best part of me? I thought it was.

I'm so freaking emotional today I don't know what to do with myself. I'm pissed at the world. The world didn't do this to me. But sure feels like it. I don't want to see, smell or hear anyone today. I'm so fucking tired of all of this bullshit called life.

page 33
This isn't living this is existing. Why do I have to relive being beaten, raped and tortured every fucking day? Was I that bad of a person really?

Who did I screw over to deserve this? These faceless men killed my baby. They might as well have cut it out of my belly. They killed the best part of me. Stole my memories. I wonder how many more they've done this to?

I can't remember their faces but I remember their stinking breath. I remember their hands. Their laughter cheering each other on to do it again. I remember their

page 34

stinking drunken bodies it makes me vomit again. I rolled out of bed screaming, crying, shaking. I need some one to talk to, someone to distract me. I'm afraid to move. It's feeling like they are always watching me.

They burned down the house after Jazz got me out.

5 have not been found. When will they find me? I can't go anywhere that I'm not hiding. They run free and I'm trapped in October in the belly of the beast

page 35

that consumes me daily. Today is Thursday. I think I ate on Monday. It really doesn't matter. I haven't slept a full night in months. If I eat it comes back up. So why bother.

The chemo burns me up. Feels like my skin is on fire. My belly is burning like someone poured gasoline down my throat and set it on fire. This is just messed up.

I throw up again but there's nothing there. It hurts like hell. I wish I would just die.

page 36

I hate what this has done to me. I hate what I've become. A million people it seems have a million different ways I should deal with this. None of these ass holes are dealing or have dealt with this. I don't give a shit how many times you've read about it until you live it yourself you don't have a fucking clue. Why don't they just shut the fuck up?

Well meaning as they think they are some days I just need them to shut the hell up and give me a hug.

page 37

God I'm so awful looking and grotesque no one wants to get that close. Except for Rae she's the only one who walks in armed with her "goodies" for me as she calls them, says not one word but comes to me, puts her arms around me kisses my forehead and just holds me. Not one word for a long time. Lets me cry or say nothing for the longest time then I hear her say softly "I love you Candy". Followed by what can I do for you today? I don't know what it would take to get this treatment

page 38

from anyone else. Rae's just the best.

I hate my reflection. I hate mirrors. I've covered them all. But I'm an emotional train wreck today.

Saw my reflection in this damn window and put my fist

through it again.

Cut my damn hand again. This is getting friggin' expensive. Off to Home Depot to buy a new one as soon as they open so I can replace this one again.

page 39
Jimmy says I have issues. Issues? No Shit? Really?

He's pissed because I woke him early. He likes to sleep until an hour before he's to be at work then wants me to call his Albuquerque ass to wake him up on time. I just needed to hear his voice someone to reassure me everything would be ok.

The ass hole yelled at me. My hand bleeding sitting on the floor. Can't get myself together from the damn nightmares then this. God I am a wreck.

page 40
Mr. Wonderful says he loves me but he hates being woke up early. Well fuck me?!

He also says his words "If you make it until December we will talk about our life together." What the fuck? Really? If? But I am to go to New Mexico for Christmas. Why?

The doc told me to use Facebook to talk to people don't shutdown.

It should be easy he said to talk to people because you never have to see them and say whatever you want.

page 41

I wonder how many times he's used his Facebook?

That's where I met Rae so it's not all bad. I met Jimmy there one night when I was at my lowest. I wasn't planning on seeing another day.

All my pill bottles. The meds- lovely meds. Pain, muscle relaxer, xanax, my fruit loop medicine all lined up in a row. Lids off. Lovely bottle of Crown Royal and a bottle of chilled wine. And the loaded .38 all by the bed.

This was gonna be the

page 42

night I showed up on Facebook in a stupor reading mindless posts from strangers. I decided to go play a little in YoVille. What the hell?

Jimmy talked to me. Talked me down he had no clue. So here I am to die another day. Jimmy became my habit, made me think he loved me. I'm so damn vulnerable so gullible. I'd listen to anything. I miss the thought of being loved but I'm afraid to see anyone face to face. I'm just fucked! My new word for my life.

page 43

I never put dates on this stupid thing it's useless. Days just roll over one another and it doesn't matter. Don't even know why I write this stupid stuff - I guess because this is a close as talking to someone I can get. I trust no one see no one. Except Rae of course. I'm just afraid I'll wake up and the rest of my life memory will be gone.

It's Mother's Day morning I need to do something to remember Mom, Jazmyn and Jimmy's mom. Off to Home Depot bought 3 weeping cherry trees planted

page 44

them by the lake. They'll be beautiful when they bloom swaying in the wind. Mom would love them.

Dumb ass Jimmy listened to a CJ clown about my pics I posted online.

He's such an idiot. Yes they are copies of online pics and from catalogs and magazines. Duh! My originals were burned. He knows that.

He just wants out so it's easier to toss me out like the trash than to stand by me. That's fine. Goodbye Jimmy Take a few more pieces of my heart.

page 45

Bex comes to the rescue takes me to Georgia. Marietta outside of Atlanta she says I've lived here before but I can't remember. It's all crazy. But then again so am I.

It's ok its fun for a little while but it gets nuts quick. Before I left Panama City the doc says chemos no good so I'm preparing to die.

It's all fucked up.

I'm done writing screw it

I'm done.

page 46

Time to write again?

Maybe?

Jim says yes!

page 47

Just when I'd given up on people Jim Clark shows up. I can't tell you the date or the time but I can tell you he showed up with a big heart.
I know I sat though hours of chemo alone because I didn't want to bother anyone. When I'm allowed to bring in my laptop, Jim steps in.

This is one man with the biggest heart of anyone I've ever met.

He talks me through the mindless hours of chemo and miserable funeral music.

page 48

I miss the beach. Jim takes photos of the beach for me. Makes videos for me, gives me my beach.

Every day I'm at chemo Jim shows up online. He makes this so much easier.

Just talk. About music, about life, about nothing in particular. Just breathe he says. He mentions hummingbird food. I know he's been here before.

He tells me he's here holding my hand. I believe him I feel him.
I am no longer alone.

page 49

He lets me talk about anything and doesn't get offended with my silly banter.

Some days I'm not so nice. Pretty crass. But he keeps showing up. Keeps holding my hand. Jim is my new addiction. I wake up just to see what he has for me today. He always finds a way to make me smile.

I received a package from Jim and couldn't stop crying for the longest time. The nicest, sweetest, most beautiful painting of my beach, no our beach.

page 50

I love this man. He is such a wonderful friend. No one has ever done such a wonderful thing for me.

He sent me my own little beach complete with sand and starfish. And the music is incredible. I've fallen in love with Tyrone Wells music. The Braxton Brothers, they are all wonderful. His sweet mom included a card and a book. I guess this wonderful kindness runs in the family.

How could someone who has never met me know me so well?

page 51

Then again it could have something to do with endless hours of me talking his ears (or eyes) off. He's easy to talk to. Such a lovely person. On days when I just don't want to go on he makes me hang on for another day. Waiting to see what he has up his sleeve for me. What new photos he's taken.

He surprises me with music. New songs to give me hope. New reasons to smile. He can always make me smile.

Some days 3 little dots . . . just make my day.

page 52

I have an idea. It's crazy I know. But that's part of who

I am. A little bit crazy. Crazy helps me survive. Crazy distracts me.
I have this little butterfly tattoo. I got it on a crazy night. Too much tequila with Jazz. What the hell was I thinking?

She got one too.

Butterflies on our boobs a sign of freedom she said but tucked away in a place it wouldn't show in our photo shoots. OMG we were nuts!

page 53
I've listened to this Tyrone Wells cd a thousand times already it seems. The songs are wonderful. The lyrics amazing.

I guess Jim and I both have some favorites.

"Need" is one of his favorites.

I need you, need you baby. Gosh if I could sing myself I'd sing it to Jim.

I'm afraid my singing would make small children cry!

How could a stranger make a crazy girl like me feel so special? And feel loved.

page 54

My God did I say that?

He makes me feel loved. But with him it's not fake. Not made up or forced it's just what it is.
He is such a wonderful friend. Friends, real friends are supposed to love each other aren't they?

Why am I questioning it? I'm such a spazz.

I should just accept it for what it is.

A crazy thing called love between two friends.

page 55

Hold on, Hold onto me...

I love this song too. That's it! I'll keep my Jim with me at all times.

I'll do it tomorrow. I'll add

Hold On . . .
to my tattoo. A reminder on my worst of days right there to remind me I'm never alone.

I'm just crazy enough to do it. I need the reminder. Damn now he'll be showering with me too!

Makes me smile, but he may think I'm insane.

page 56

Won't be the first time a man has thought that. Probably won't be the last.
Did it! Tattooed the tit! Geez these meds are good today but I still can't write worth a shit!

HOLD ON . . .

Tattooed there. Feeling no pain.

Morphine sweet freakin' morphine.

Used as a last resort but I just couldn't take the pain anymore today.

page 57

I love Jim. He can look past all my bullshit and find my truth.

I tell him I'm ok. He says he wants me to be better than ok. He takes me to the beach again and again. Now it's our beach. God I miss it but he brings me home to it every day.

I hate Georgia. I'm miserable. Bex is drinking more and more. Becoming more agitated with me.

She came into my room drunk and asked me

page 58

"Why don't you go ahead and fucking die already?"

This isn't the Bex I know.

I'm killing her with this thing that consumes me. It's now consuming her. It does everyone that cares about me. Eventually they all leave. My God I don't want to hurt anyone this way. I don't want to hurt Jim and Rae like this.

I would rather die a thousand deaths than

page 59

to hurt them. They have both been so good to me.

Rae has taken care of me like more than a friend. She reminds me of my mom. Picking me up, cleaning up my nosebleeds after chemo. And omg all the times I've puked on her. Has she complained? Not once.

Jim keeps me sane. Keeps me happy. Makes sure I've eaten. I can't lie to him or pass it off he just always knows. He has his own built in Candy Bullshit Detector. He knows me better than anyone.

page 60

Jim's off on a business trip. I've given him a little tease about the tattoo. Will he think I'm a total fruitcake? I guess today will tell.

I'm posting a photo of it. Stupid camera phone. Needs a better operator.

Jim should take the pic. All of his photos turn out fabulous.

This damn thing - the dots look like freakin' squares wtf?
Oh well - posting it. Jim's at a meeting. We'll see if he notices.

page 61
He may like it or just think my "Cheese has completely slid of my cracker" as Jazz used to say.

Time will tell. I'll just sit and wait. Like I've got other things to do yeah, right!

Facebook I love freakin' Facebook that's where my real friends were found.

Well here goes. He's on during his meeting - tisk tisk Mr. Clark cheating work? Wtf cares.

page 62
Jim says "Is this for real?"

Uh oh - did I screw up?

He likes it! Says I made him smile.

Well it's about time the tables were turned.

Gone back to his meeting but will talk to me later.

Of course he will he always does.

I hate this damn place. I wish I'd never left Florida but I've made my bed and here I am.

page 63

I'm so sick today. Death can't come soon enough. So tired of the pain. My feet are so swollen. I can't walk today. My bones hurts. There's not one thing on me that doesn't make me want to scream.

My head is killing me. It won't stop. It's excruciating. I can't say anything to Bex it will just piss her off.

She tells me she can't stand to look at me anymore. She's drunk again. My lip is busted and my eye is black and swollen from things she's thrown

page 64

at me. She's slapped me at least a dozen times. I won't tell Jim this part he worries about me enough. I want to go home. Bex has broken so many things, there is glass everywhere. I've never seen her this bad or heard her talk like this. She wants everyone out of her house. She wants me to die bitch die.

My God what have I done? I'm afraid of what will happen next.

I'll talk to Jim. Be careful of how much I

page 65

tell him. Don't want him to worry too much.

His Candy BS Detector is always on anyway. That's just Jim.
Packing my bags only 2 don't have much. My painting, a few books and my beach, meds and shake mix.

As soon as she's in her room I'm out the door. Feeling weak but I can't take this cruel drama anymore. She's lost her mind.

page 66

Safe at the Hampton Inn.

Jacuzzi woohoo!

Where's Jim when I need him tonight?

Online waiting to see if I'm ok of course.

Always with me no matter what.

In the morning I'll make some calls and find a place to go.

Jim say come home. If nothing else I can crash at his place. That's so... Jim!

page 67

Always taking care of me. Either way I'm clearing out my bank account and picking up medical records.

I'm heading home one way or another. I've been so miserable here. I'm ready. Mom and Pops have a con-do waiting.

Jim says he could drive up this way. Rae says she'll come or will meet me in Dothan. Jim offers again.

I think I can make it just take my time. If I get tired I'll just stop and rest. I have to do this one on my own. I need to do this.

page 68

Heading to Florida. I'm so happy!

For so long I stressed over not knowing where home was.

Now I know. Home is where you leave your heart at the end of the day. Home is where you want to be when the whole world just sucks. Such profound words Ha Ha.

The closer I am to Jim and Rae the closer I am to home.

page 69

Haven't been gone long and already another stop...

Not gonna stress I'm on my way. If it takes me a week I don't care I' going home! I will feel even closer to Rae and Jim.

I'm just gonna crawl up in their hearts and stay. It's safe and comfortable there. It's the only place I feel like I belong.

They always make room for me there. I'm going home.

Happy Dance!!!

page 70
I love Mickey D's

Free wifi and they sell happiness in a cup. It's called Mocha Frappe'

Happylooyah!!

This is my 3rd

did I mention I gotta go pee? BRB dear journal

doing the potty dance

Yes I'm nuts can't believe a 30 year old just wrote that down. OMG that either.

page 71

I don't care I'm happy as a clam, light as a feather on my way to Florida, life's getting better, gonna talk to Jim nibble on his ear. Can't wait to be close to him can't wait to feel him near.

Ok seriously I gotta go pee and get back on the road.

Ok back on the road let's get me home. Cancer you'll have to take a ride in the trunk today I've got no time for your chit today!

page 72

OMG please help me make it home.

Just changed a little grandmas tire on the interstate. Dickhead men wouldn't offer to help. That's ok it's done and she's on her way.

I'm feeling pretty lousy nausea is overwhelming. Talked to Jim again I'll be ok. He can't know how bad I really feel or he'll be on the road all I gotta do is say the word. But I need to do this for myself.

page 73

Hathaway Bridge lights never looked so wonderful to me it was like a Welcome Home Candy sign.

Damn I'm tired. But I'm so wired from the caffeine ugh! I'm home. Condo home. Florida home. Rae's already called and Jim's online. All is right with the world one more day.

I love the beach. The sound, the smell and the feel. God I want to go for a run but my skinny ass is drained and tired now if my f'n mind will shut up!

page 74
Jill Scott
A Long Walk.

Good Song, Great Idea

Long walk on the beach

I'm back!
What
The
Hell
Was
I
Thinking?

That was a long ass walk! But it was good.

page 75
Need a shower then a nap. Damn I hurt. My hip is kill-ing me.

Where's Jim? Rub my hip. Damn I know he would. Why am I such a spazz?

The only man in the world I know won't hurt me and I won't let him see me. Not his fault God knows he tries. I don't mean to seem cruel. I just can't stand the thought of looking into one more persons eyes that I'll have to say goodbye to. Especially his eyes. God I love his eyes. I love Jim. What I wouldn't give to snuggled up in his arms tonight.

page 76

I'm such an idiot. I would love to just take one walk on the beach, our beach, with him, watch the sunset and just hold onto him until I fall asleep.

One things for sure. There would be no nightmares. He would find a way to keep them away.

I would drift off to sleep just breathing him in. Listening to his heart beat. Listening to his breathing. Just feeling safe in his arms. Damn I love this man.

What am I doing? Dreaming

page 77

He always tells me he loves me. And he makes me believe him. No I believe him period. He is good for my soul. Good for my spirit. He's just good for me period.

Can't get him out of my mind.

Can't wait to see him online.

Can't wait for a hell.

I am so lucky to have him in my life.

I'm crazy I know but let a dying girl have her dream. It's just a dream but omg what a dream!

page 78
Father's Day!

Every Father's Day since I can remember I mourned the loss of my father. The man died when I was so very young.

Today Pops brought me a letter from the lawyers.

My father is alive and well. An executive at a large corporation.

His letter has a check for $25,000 in it. All I have to do is never contact him he says mom and I ruined his life.

page 79
He tells me, his daughter that I am vomit from his past. I need to be washed away from his memory to take the money and leave him alone.

What the fuck? I didn't know he existed. How the hell did I ruin his life? He has lived well while mom and I struggled to keep food in the house, a roof over our heads and lights on.

I feel something I've not felt it's hate and I don't like it. Disgust. He makes me want to vomit and I do. I'm really sick now.

page 80

He never once made an effort to contact me. The lawyers hired a private investigator to find any family I might have. I wish he had stayed dead. I am nothing to him and he makes me feel less than nothing.

Fuck him and his money.

Let's get drunk and burn this mother fucker.

I watch the check and his letter burn, it feels good.

I'm not for sale.

page 81

Jim again is here for me through this. I've made such an ass of myself. I just want to disappear but he won't let me.

Why does he put up with my insanity?

He must really care or he's completely nuts like me.

He just cares he's such a good man.

My own father wouldn't walk across the street to see me but Jim tries everyday.

Jim finds good in me when I feel lower than dirt. No eloquent words can I find. My so called father isn't worthy to shine his shoes.

page 82

Another letter today from the attorneys much like came before but this one comes with dread. What more could it be right? I'm so sick today I can't keep anything down. I feel weak. Don't need anymore surprises but it's probably nothing.

Breathe Candy just breathe. That's what Jim would say. Nothing could top the last letter anyway.
Ok maybe I'm not ready yet. Try to sip on a shake and pull myself together, then open it.

page 83

.... - (A) 28
.... - (M) 26
.... - (N) 26
.... - (B) 24
.... - (Z) 21

L and B ran their own catering company.

M is an engineer

N is a nurse

Z is in college works for an advertising agency and is working on a Business degree

These are my siblings. Just when I thought there could be no more surprises. Boom! Here we go.

My dead father has 5 more children.

page 84

His wife didn't know I existed until she intercepted the attorneys letter. She then told the children who now want to know their big sister.

WTF? This is too much, I'm so overwhelmed I don't know how to feel.

I hate him more. I don't like this feeling. I can't sink to his level.

This is killing me. They want to know me, want to talk to me the sooner the better they say. I can't do this.

page 85

Their letter is kind. Jim is right none of us have anything to do with the way our so-called father has treated any of us.

It's not their fault.

How can I introduce myself to them? I'm dying, I feel it everyday. I try to push it aside but it eats away at me every day. How can I say hello to them, get to know them and tell them ok the jokes on you 'cause I'm dying. Goodbye.

How cruel is all of this?

I'm so torn I don't

page 86

know what to do or how to feel.

Jim says put it away. Breathe. Don't let it overwhelm me. Too Late! Breathe he repeats. I don't have to do anything he says to me. That's good because I have no clue where to start.

God I'm so confused.

The chemo burns inside me I'm so sick, now this. God what have I done? Why are you punishing me? Is this just a cruel joke.

page 87

Nothing is funny. I wish the earth would open up and swallow me. I want to disappear.

If I wasn't such an idiot.

If I wasn't so afraid.

If I wasn't so afraid of just looking into those eyes and having to say goodbye, today would be the day I would find Jim. Wish I could run into his arms and just stay there where it's safe. Where I don't feel so alone. So isolated. God just to feel some ones arms around me again. Someone I could trust. I could trust Jim with my life. What the hell is wrong with me?

page 88

I have no lucid thoughts today. All I can do is cry. Once again this sperm donor of a father of mine has reduced me to a child. How can a man father children and be so cruel? He says I am the vomit from his past. Today that's exactly how I feel. I am vomit. I am worthless useless garbage taking up space. When Jim asks me how I am today I will say I'm ok. Let's hope his bullshit detector is not on. There's no sense dumping this on him today. I've dumped enough

page 89

of my drama on him. He has a life and doesn't need this.

OMG he wants to talk. What do I say my mics not working? Can't lie to him. I'll just tell him I can't right now maybe later. I hate lying. It's not me.

Some lies are meant to protect. Mom I'm not angry

with you now I understand. Forgive me for being angry. You never did anything but love me. You were my mom, dad and best friend. I understand, it's ok. I love you.

page 90

Jim what would I do without you? You get me through another day and give me hope. Make me smile. Make me know I'm not alone anymore. You love me. You always tell me you love me. You make me laugh. You make me smile. You give me strength when I have none. You put back pieces of this ragged old crushed heart. You ease my mind. You give me peace. You tell me you are here holding my hand during chemo. I know you are. I feel you here. I feel your heart.

page 91

Night has come and I'm so sick again. God will this never end? Stood in the shower 4 times today just letting the cold water fall on me. This chemo just burns me inside. Maybe I am crazy. I feel as though I'm losing my mind. Wish I could sleep. I'm exhausted. Can't eat, can't sleep. Dropped 5lbs this week. That's not good. I got down to 95lbs when I was in Georgia. Can't do that again. Wish I could sleep to escape.

page 92

page 93   Blank (just a scribble to get ink flowing again)

page 94

Nothing else matters but love.

I wanted to fill every page with the wonderful things you've done for me. Fill it with all the fun stuff, with all the things that made me laugh and made me smile. But there's not enough time.

page 95   Blank

page 96

My handwriting is horrible these days but I hope you can figure out what's here.

Don't think about the sadness or all of the bad things that have happened along the way.

But please my dearest Jim remember me with a smile. You've put countless smiles on my face and made me laugh out loud.

Where my heart only know sorrow you filled it with the joy of knowing you!

page 97   Blank

page 98

You have been my rock.

My hand to hold.

My shoulder to lean on.

My confidant.

You've listened and you stayed when the rest walked away.

I will never forget you. I will carry you in my heart for an eternity.

page 99   Blank

page 100

I finally know what real love is. Today you said it best. Love is a feeling we get inside when everything just feels right. When it brings a tear to your eye even when you are happy.

page 101   Blank

page 102

You filled many lonely nights with the comfort of knowing I wasn't alone. You made this place feel like my home simply because I feel closer to you here. I've found in you that one true friend that I was missing.

page 103 Blank

page 104

Please always know there hasn't been a moment since I've met you that I haven't loved you. The thought of you. Or just the mention of your name. Whenever you go I will be there hiding somewhere in your heart because that's the best place to be.

page 105   Blank

page 106

I'll be there on the beach and in the rain and in the music that you filled my heart with. A part of me will always be here because this is where I belong.

page 107   Blank

page 108

My regret is I was a coward. I couldn't look you in your beautiful eyes that just make me melt. Yes they do,

To say thank you is so inadequate. To say I love you goes on forever. That won't stop.

page 109   Blank

page 110

I know it's time for me to go very soon. I won't, can't say goodbye. Please forgive me for all I've put you through, I know it hasn't been easy.

page 111   Blank

page 112

I love you Jim.

You are always in my thoughts.

You have been the smile that was unexplainable.

That crazy laugh out loud when I was alone.

Please always know
there hasn't been a
moment since I've
met you that I
haven't loved you.
the thought of you.
Or just the mention
of your name
Wherever you go I
will be there hiding
somewhere in your
heart because that's the best place
I could be

You have been my strength.

My comfort.

page 113   Blank

page 114

You have been my love.

I will love you long after I leave here.

Is eternity enough?

I hope one day soon you will find that one who loves you the way you deserve to be loved.

page 115   Blank

page 116

Remember me and smile.

That's all I want.

My heart breaks because I know it's almost time to leave.

I never meant to hurt anyone while I was here.

I only wanted to love and be loved.

page 117   Blank

page 118

Listen to our songs.

Walk on our beach.

I'll be there waiting for you always.

If I know nothing else I know one thing.

I have been loved.

page 119   Blank

page 120

Keep smiling my sweet Jim.

I'm with you always just as you are with me.
I finally truly have been loved.

page 121   Blank

page 122

I love you my Jim.

I will see you one day.

Time may stop but love never ends.

I'll love you forever,

Candy xo

page 123   Blank

page 124

Today's the day I let it all go the anger, frustration,

disappointment, embarrassment, the hurt, the pain, the sickness, the nightmares.

I will remember things that need to be remembered. Forget things that need to forgotten.

I will take with me those that love me. Leave behind those that hurt me. My sadness will be replaced with joy. My heart once broken will be full of only love. I will run like I have never run before. I will dance for joy. I will sing because my heart is overflowing with love.

page 125   Blank

page 126

I will kiss the face of Jesus then bow at his feet. I will thank my Heavenly Father for his love, his mercy, his grace.

No more will I be lonely or sad. No more will I be in pain. My heart will be finally free to dance among the stars. My soul for once can rejoice and be at peace. I'm letting go of my yesterday and all of their misery. I'm holding on to my eternity and it's joy.

I have been loved. I have been cherished. I will go on in the hearts of those who love me.

page 127   Blank

page 128

I will remain in the sands on the beach.

I will be in the tide that runs to the shore and tickle the toes of my friends.

I will be in the soft gentle rain that kisses the cheeks of those I love and there with them I will dance and laugh.

I will be the butterfly who shows up unannounced to bring a smile on fluttering wings.

I will be in the seashells by the shore to be held and adored.

page 129   Blank

page 130

I will remain in the music that I love that reaches your heart when nothing else can.

I will be in the soft gentle breeze that passes by you. Do you feel me?

I will be in the laughter of the child. Do you hear me?

I will be in the tender embrace of those who love you. Do you feel your arms around me let me hold you in my heart.

page 131   Blank

page 132

It was so nice to talk to you last night.

I needed to hear your voice once more.

It always comforts me.

You always make me feel at peace no matter what is going on.

I love you laughter and your smile.

I wish there were real words to describe what it all means to me.

page 133   Blank

page 134

Thank you for sharing that big thing called your heart with me. It's amazing to find a place for me there. But I have felt the warmth of your caring heart in this ugly dark place I have sometimes been. You've made this load lighter that I carry. My days so much brighter.

page 135   Blank

page 136

My breathing is a little more difficult today.

I know it won't be much longer now.

But Jim it's really ok.

I had a dream again about my baby, my mom and Jazmyn.

They are waiting for me.

It will be wonderful to hold my little one in my arms. She has always

page 137   Blank

page 138

been in my heart. I'm a terrible person you know? I never even dared to dream of giving her a name.

So much is missing. But soon I will be complete.

You have filled in so much that has been missing from my heart and life.

page 139   Blank

page 140

The music.

The incredible music.

You know my heart and soul. Every day the music has kept me going. Soothes my soul. Makes me so happy. Finally someone who "gets" me! Wonderful you! My sweet Jim.

page 141   Blank

page 142

My choices of music have always been odd to most. But I've always loved music. It's brave enough to say what you can't. The window to your soul mom always said. Bit you know this already you get it.

How can people get through their lives without music?

page 143   Blank

page 144

I've wanted to go back through the links I've used and write them down. But I haven't. Guess I've just been lazy that way. I think by now you know how I feel. You know where to find it all. Jim dear you are my music. Are you smiling? You'd better be!

page 145   Blank

page 146

I hope you will have pleasant memories of me. I hope you smile. Yes I was chicken chit in a lot of ways. But I'm sure you heard me thinking out loud! You have made my life fun. I've never laughed so much, smiled so much or loved so much.

page 147   Blank

page 148

Try not to be so sad when I'm gone. Limit those friggin' tears. I've cried enough for everyone on earth.

Celebrate the wonderful moments in my life. There have been those. My greatest was when God placed

you Jim dear, in my life!

page 149 Blank

page 150

Take your behind on over to Quig's... Have a couple of chocolate martinis for us.

Yes I want one!!

Smile, laugh, play.

Remember the crazy girl who hid everything except her heart from you.

You know it inside out.

page 151 Blank

page 152

I'll never fill this all the way but just know my heart is overflowing with things I want to say and want you to know but don't know how to put it into words.

Yes dear, I know you would say it's ok

Yes dear, I know you love me.

Yes dear, I know it's all going to be alright.

page 153 Blank

page 154

Turn on the music.

You know I'll be listening too.

Did you think I'd just go away and not be here to bug you? Naw... Not me.

I've got you in my heart.

Above my heart and on my pink toes! . . .

I've surrounded my self in you.

Because you are what gets me through.

page 155
Thank you for making my bitter days sweet!

page 156
You are my drug of choice.

Jim Clark = Candy Crack

Wouldn't change a thing I get so tired these days.

But when I turn on our music or just get a short chance to say hello to you.

Everything is better.

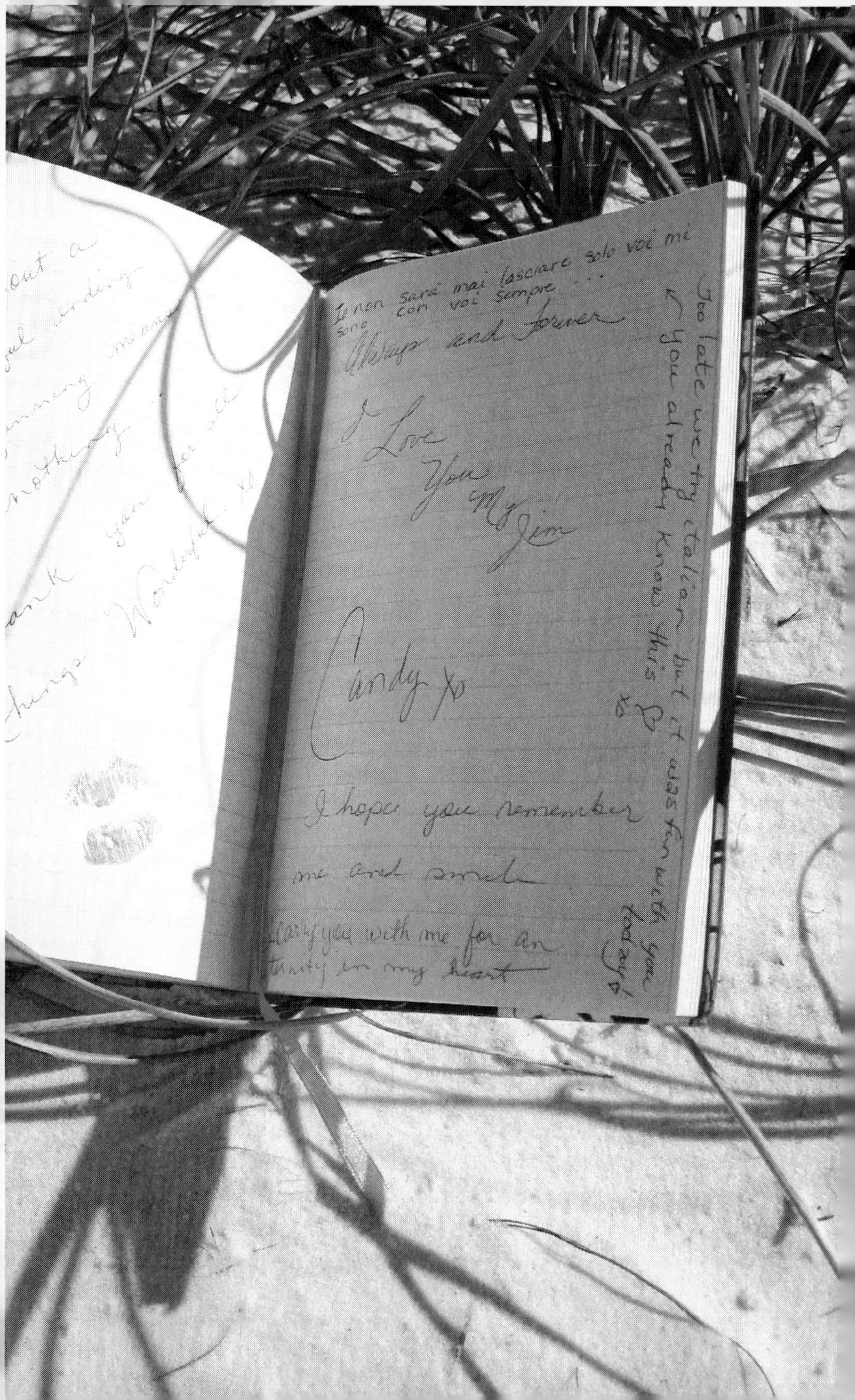
Io non sarò mai lasciare solo voi mi sono con voi sempre . . .
Always and forever
I Love You My Jim
Candy xo
I hope you remember me and smile
carry you with me for an
in my heart
Too late we try italian but it was fun with you
You already know this ♡ xo

I love you!

You know it by now don't you!

No?
Well Dayum Jim get a clue! LOL :)

page 157 Blank

page 158

I'm as slow as a snail so the choice of the candy dish is definitely me. I hope with every little clink of the dish you smile. It's nothing significant, nothing big. But it's silly just like me.

Smile Jim Dear

:)

page 159 Blank

page 160

I don't know why I been blessed to have you and Rae in my life. But I'm so grateful for it. I hope you and Rae continue to be friends for years to come. Once you really get to know her you'll find how great she really is. You both have my heart. I love you so much.

page 161 Blank

page 162

Ok I've been writing for a while. So I'll stop for now. If I don't write one more word let me end with what I

know to be true. Jim dear, now and then, always and forever. I love you.

Candy xo

page 163   Blank

page 164

Today is a difficult day. It's hard to breathe. My head hurts beyond belief, everything hurts. This is no longer living it's existing in a body I no longer know. I spent most of last night in bed or sitting on the floor trying to find a comfortable position. Another restless night. I managed to sleep about an hour somewhere between 2 and 4. I dreamed. No nightmares this time.

page 165   Blank

page 166

The dream was wonderful. Very sweet. So Jim. For a little while I was in a place I wanted to be. Safe, happy and smiling. You hold me. We danced. We loved. A dream to treasure. And then I woke up to reality. The reality that this could very well be my last day here. And I think back at how I spent my last night here.

page 167   Blank

page 168

Frustrated and angry at him.

Snapping at Grace.

Complaining and bitching about him. The one who makes me feel less than nothing. What was I thinking? I hate to think my last night was spent being upset, angry and crying and dumping it all on you.

You know you hate the word but I am truly so very sorry.

I love you Jim and I don't want our last conversation to be about him.

page 169   Blank

page 170

Monday night was the sweetest night of my life.

It was love. It was music. It was you. It was smiles. Laughter.
Kisses. And more love. It was you letting me know you would keep me in your heart.

I laughed. I cried. I never wanted to leave.
I never thought for one moment I could feel so much love.
My heart overflows. And I watched it over again 4 more times just so I could see your face, hear your voice.

This thing is crazy. It's unexplainable. It's nothing I was looking for but something that found me and completely took me by surprise.

page 171

Thank you for holding me. I felt every moment of you here with me. xo

page 172

It's bizarre, completely insane and I wouldn't trade one second of it.

I don't know when it happened.

Don't think I even realized what has really happened until I started writing.

If I don't know anything else.

If I forget my name or don't take one more breath.

I know that I love you.

No reservations.

You are my heart treasure.

I only wish I had longer in a better body.

But I can't put into words what you mean to me.

My God man, I love you!

page 173   Blank

page 174

I can't wait to hear your voice or see your face or see those 3 little dots show up online.

Can't wait to see "hey you ..." or "hello beautiful" to show up on the screen. It's the highlight of my day

My heart jumps for joy and I smile.

I smile because you are here and I no longer feel alone.

However we happened I'm so glad we did.

I wouldn't have missed one moment with you for anything.

I'm so tired now but I can't tell you enough how much I love you Jim.

I'll watch you one more time for today and if I leave

page 175

Jim,

I was dead inside you brought me back to life now I will live forever!

Because of you.

page 176

this world today.

It's ok.

Nothing that's been done to me can take away what my heart feel of course.

With the last breath I take I will know that I am loved.

Love survives anything.

It's the one thing that can't be taken away.

I'll carry you always in my heart.

Saving a seat next to me just for you.

Don't be in a hurry.

You've much to do.

I'll see you soon and nothing or no one will ever stand in the way again and that's a promise.

page 177

Without a wonderful ending the beginning means nothing . . .

Thank you for all things wonderful.

xo

(lipstick kiss on page)

page 178

**Io non sara mai lasciare solo voi mi
sono con voi sempre . . .**

**Too late we try Italian but it was fun with you today.
You already know this xo**

Always and Forever

I love you my Jim

Candy xo

I hope you remember me and smile.

I carry you me for an eternity in my heart.

page 179   Blank

page 180

**If given the chance to do it all over again, even going
through all of this...**

**I would gladly do it to spend one more hour hearing
your voice and seeing your smile.**

It would be worth every moment to me.

**I hope you find the love that you so deserve. The love
that takes you by surprise, overwhelms you, comforts
you and cares for you every moment as you have made**

me feel. xo

page 181
ti amo molto

Sempre e persempre

(lipstick kiss)

inside back cover
No matter what happens always know I love you and I'm here.

Love remains and hearts heal.

I know.

You healed mine.

Candy
xo

THANK YOU

GOD

Thank you Lord for letting me stay on earth long enough to meet many people, to make friends and to enjoy the friendships I have made. Every day is a gift from you.

JAMES EARL CLARK

Thank you Dad for instilling your values into me. I respect your work ethic as well as your wonderful dry sense of humor. You taught me to stay calm even when things around me get crazy. You introduced me to music and it keeps me dancing.

HAZEL JEFFORD CLARK

Thank you Mom for raising all of us kids and still making it fun. Thanks for the use of your photos in here. You helped me develop my love for photography and made it one of my favorite things to do. I will always be your little "Jimmy" and forever love you.

TAYLOR STEVEN CLARK

Thank you Taylor for being just like me, except that you can play the music I always wanted to learn how to play. You helped me appreciate living in the moment, having fun with friends, doing nothing, hanging out, and to enjoy the little things in life.

LINDSEY JACQUELINE CLARK

Thank you Linz for not being afraid of being creative in both art and relationships. You make me smile when I see my stubbornness come out in you. I love the way you love the cute, fluffy, colorful, and all things different around you.

MARA RODRIGUEZ

My "CPR" editor who took time away from her family and friends to help me get this "project", as she calls it, completed without my "that" word being used a million times. Thank you for your dedication, encouraging words, and patience with me.

JESSI MILLER ~ JAKE MEYER

My friends Jessi and Jake, who are there for me when I need them. Jessi encourages me to be creative and to keep a positive attitude. Jake is there for me when I need a laugh, a break from work or to just talk about guy stuff. Love you guys and thanks.

xOxOxOx

xo

SUGGESTED LINKS

THE AMERICAN CANCER SOCIETY ~ www.cancer.org
Saving lives by helping people stay well, get well, find cures, and fight back.
The American Cancer Society (ACS) saves lives and creates a world with less
cancer and more birthdays by helping people stay well, helping people get
well, by finding cures, and by fighting back.

LOCKS OF LOVE ~ www.locksoflove.org
A public non-profit organization that provides hairpieces to financially dis-
advantaged children in the United States and Canada under age 21 suffering
from long-term medical hair loss from any diagnosis. The prostheses they
provide help to restore their self-esteem and their confidence, enabling them
to face the world and their peers.

HOSPICE ~ www.hospicenet.org
Hospice care is provided to patients who have a limited life expectancy.
Although most hospice patients are cancer patients, hospices accept anyone
regardless of age or type of illness. These patients have also made a decision
to spend their last months at home or in a homelike setting.

NATIONAL DOMESTIC VIOLENCE ~ www.thehotline.org
Help your friend or family member recognize the abuse. Tell him or her you
see what is going on and that you want to help. Help them recognize that what
is happening is not "normal" and that they deserve a healthy, non-violent relationship. Call their 24-hour National Domestic Violence Hotline at 1-800-799-
SAFE (7233) or TTY 1-800-787-3224 to discuss your concerns and questions.

FACEBOOK ~ www.facebook.com
Facebook is a social utility that connects people with friends and others who
work, study and live around them. Facebook helps you connect and share
with the people in your life. Find me and add me ~ http://www.facebook.
com/Ad3.org